FREIGHT CARS
OF THE '40s AND '50s

Jeff Wilson

KALMBACH BOOKS

Kalmbach Books
21027 Crossroads Circle
Waukesha, Wisconsin 53186
www.Kalmbach.com/Books

Published in 2015
19 18 17 16 15   1 2 3 4 5

Manufactured in China

ISBN: 978-1-62700-144-1
EISBN: 978-1-62700-145-8

Editor: Randy Rehberg
Book Design: Tom Ford, Patti Keipe

Unless noted, photographs were taken by the author.

Library of Congress Control Number: 2014958386

Contents

Southern Pacific class SP-3 4-10-2 no. 5044 is in the twilight of its career as it leads an extra freight past the depot at Jefferson, Ore., in July 1953. Tucked behind the tender is a Pennsylvania Railroad X-29 boxcar, followed by a variety of AAR boxcars of different heights, several tank cars, and some refrigerator cars. *Robert Milner*

Transition-era freight cars

The two-decade period from 1940 through 1960, when railroads were making the transition from steam to diesel locomotives, has become known as the transition era. And the transition era remains among the most popular time frames for modelers to set their layouts.

Railroad equipment, technology, and operations changed significantly during this time. The most obvious change was at the head end of trains.

In 1940, steam locomotives powered almost all freight trains. Diesels could be found in yard service and pulling streamlined passenger trains, but only a few mainline diesels headed freight trains.

By 1950, diesels were everywhere, relegating steam locomotives to secondary trains, branch lines, and scrapyards.

In 1960, the steam era officially ended, as the last non-excursion steam locomotives turned their last miles on Class 1 railroads on the Norfolk & Western, Illinois Central, and Grand Trunk Western.

Freight cars also changed significantly during this time. In 1940, the nation's freight car fleet was an aging collection of equipment. Although some new steel cars were on the rails, the Depression had taken its toll on freight cars as railroads relied on older refurbished wood equipment. By the 1950s, fleets of new steel cars of many types were serving railroads across the country.

By the end of the 1950s, freight cars were becoming larger, with 70-ton-capacity cars replacing 40- and 50-ton cars. The ubiquitous 40-foot, general-service boxcar was on the decline, as specialized 50-foot cars with cushion underframes, insulated boxcars, and cars with special loading racks and equipment were becoming the norm. Other types of cars, such as covered hoppers and piggyback flatcars, were increasing in number and importance.

Variety

A tremendous drawing point in modeling this era is that you can choose freight cars from hundreds of railroads. During the transition era there were more than 100 Class 1 railroads in the United States and Canada, plus many short lines and hundreds of private car owners. Any given general freight train provided a smorgasbord of road names and paint schemes.

This book focuses on the freight cars produced and operated during this influential railroading period. Although many dramatic changes were happening in railroading as the 1950s turned into the '60s, we'll stick to a cutoff date of December 31, 1959—high-cube boxcars, 89-foot auto racks, and jumbo covered hoppers will have to wait for another volume.

There is no way a book of this size can provide complete coverage of all the freight car variations that ran during this era, so for those of you looking for more detailed information, specific railroad variations, and rosters of car types, there is an extensive list of sources on pages 93–95.

CHAPTER ONE

Modeling a freight car fleet

Putting together a fleet of freight cars for a model railroad can be a daunting task. Many variables come into play, including the railroad that you're modeling, the type of traffic your railroad handles, the era and specific year you model, and the level of fidelity and realism you're trying to attain.

Many modelers consider it part of the fun of modeling to keep their selection of freight cars as close as possible to the time frame they model. For these prototype modelers, it's of prime importance to know what cars are appropriate for a specific railroad or for a private owner at a given time.

Freight trains of the transition era were marked by strings of boxcars and reefers of varying heights in assorted shades of dark red and brown, with occasional orange and yellow reefers mixed in. This Illinois Central train is seen near Waterloo, Iowa, in March 1955. The IC hauled a lot of meat reefers on its Iowa Division through the 1950s. *Robert Milner*

This view of a Chicago yard in 1942 shows a nice variety of freight cars, including a Pennsy X-29 steel boxcar (center), a string of Milwaukee Road composite gondolas hauling coal, several ARA and AAR steel boxcars, many single-sheathed boxcars of various designs (in differing heights and shades of brown and red), a few bright yellow (and some not-so-bright yellow) refrigerator cars, and two black Sinclair tank cars (at the back). *Library of Congress*

Fidelity to specific prototypes is a key factor. For example, all 40-foot steel boxcars are not the same (as chapter 3 shows). They varied in height; their type of trucks, ends, doors, and roofs; and the basic construction used (such as straight-sill vs. tabbed-sill sideframes).

Say you want to model 1946. All-steel cars were the norm by then, but you'll still need lots of wood-sheathed boxcars as well. But don't plan on having any Pullman-Standard PS-1 boxcars (they didn't appear until 1947), Airslide covered hoppers (1954), or mechanical refrigerator cars (1949).

How about 1954? OK, now you can have a couple of those distinctive Airslide cars—but they shouldn't be weathered much. You can also have some PS-1 boxcars and a mechanical reefer or two, but no frameless tank cars (one experimental car was built that year), and no piggyback cars lettered for Trailer Train (not until 1955).

Determining how many and what types of freight cars to run, and in what percentage, is an exercise that's more of an art than a science. Tied to that task is figuring out how many home-road cars you should use in proportion to foreign-road cars—and of foreign-road cars, how many should be from neighboring roads, other major railroads, or random railroads from across the country.

You can, of course, take this task to whatever level you choose. Having the information and understanding of how and why various cars evolved will greatly increase the realism of your modeling. Let's start with a look at standard freight car types and then see how cars moved around the country.

USRA, ARA, and AAR standard cars

Early in the 1900s, railroads and manufacturers largely built cars to their own designs. The first major attempt at standardization came with the United States Railroad Administration's (USRA) temporary takeover of the country's railroads from 1917 to 1920. Part of the USRA's plan for streamlining operations and performance was adopting a series of standard locomotive and freight car designs that could be used by any manufacturer.

The USRA directed the construction of about 100,000 boxcars, hoppers, and gondolas to be distributed to a number of railroads. In addition, for several years after USRA control ended, railroads ordered thousands of additional cars to USRA or similar designs.

Individual railroads and manufacturers continued to design their own cars, but by the transition era, most cars (especially boxcars)

were being built to common standard designs approved by the American Association of Railroads (AAR) or its predecessor (until 1932), the American Railway Association (ARA).

As you'll find in the following chapters, even cars built to a standard design often featured variations in many components, including trucks, ends, roofs, doors, and brake gear.

Transition-era freight cars were built by a number of manufacturers. The two largest builders were American Car & Foundry (which became ACF Industries after 1954) and Pullman-Standard. Other major builders of the era included Bethlehem, Canadian Car & Foundry, General American, Greenville, Magor, Mount Vernon Car Shops, Pacific Car & Foundry, and Pressed Steel Car Co.

In addition, many railroads built and rebuilt cars in their own shops. These cars could feature homebuilt components, but often railroads used complete kits or major parts supplied by ACF, Pullman, and other manufacturers.

Wandering cars

A basic premise of the American rail network is that cars can be freely interchanged among all common-carrier railroads. For example, watching a 75-car freight train roll by on the Rock Island in 1950, you might see 30

A westbound Southern Pacific extra freight behind F units winds along the Sacramento River near Dunsmuir, Calif., in 1953. The train includes three flatcars hauling lumber, several double-door boxcars, and a Pennsy X-29 boxcar. Road names include SP, Pennsylvania, Illinois Central, Seaboard Air Line, Santa Fe, Central of New Jersey, and New York Central. *W. E. Malloy Jr.*

Rock Island boxcars, another 20 cars from various neighboring railroads, 10 cars from far-flung lines across the U.S. or Canada, perhaps a few refrigerator cars from Pacific Fruit Express, and possibly some tank cars from various private owners.

Freight cars can go on extensive trips off-line. For example, a car loaded on the Northern Pacific in Montana might travel to Minneapolis on the NP, be interchanged to the Chicago, Burlington & Quincy for the trip to Chicago, and then go on the Belt Railway of Chicago to the Pennsylvania Railroad to its final destination in Ohio.

A 1956 Pullman-Standard advertisement provides a good illustration of how far a freight car could roam (and how often it could be interchanged). The ad commemorated the 10th anniversary of the company's first PS-1 standard boxcar built, Lehigh Valley no. 62000. Compiled from the ad, the chart on page 12 shows that the car barely spent a

third of 1954 on the Lehigh Valley, including two- and three-month stints away from home rails.

The beauty of this practice is that it allows modelers to run many types of freight cars from a wide variety of railroads along with those of any specific railroad or railroads being modeled. And since the transition era precluded the huge merger movement that began in the 1960s, there was a tremendous variety of railroads to choose from—129 Class 1 railroads were operating in 1955.

AAR car service and per diem rules

Railroads must follow AAR rules called the *Code of Car Service* when loading cars. The exact wording of these rules has changed over the years, but the basic idea remains the same: get cars headed toward their home railroads. The following is a greatly simplified summary of the code's 18 rules as they existed in 1955 (taken

from the April 1955 *Official Railway Equipment Register*).

The intent of the code is found in Rule 1, which states, "Home cars shall not be used for the movement of traffic beyond the limits of the home road when the use of other suitable cars under these rules is practicable."

Foreign-road cars should be used for such shipments—but which ones? Per Rule 3, a foreign-road car should be loaded to a destination on the owner's line if possible; otherwise, it should go to a destination that involves the owner's line for part of the haul. Failing that, the car should be used for a load that takes it closer to its home road. If multiple suitable cars are available, the cars farthest from their home roads should be used first. If no loads are available, the car should be delivered empty to its owner (generally, via the reverse route from which it traveled while loaded). The AAR divides the country into a series of zones that specify where and how cars should be routed.

Mechanical refrigerator cars began to appear around 1950. Although limited in use, they grew in number by the end of the 1950s. This roller-bearing-equipped Santa Fe 50-foot car was built in 1959. *Santa Fe*

By the mid-1950s, general-purpose boxcars were giving way to cars equipped with loading devices (such as Evans Damage-Free "DF" loaders) and cushion underframes. *Santa Fe*

Your model fleet should represent the traffic being handled. Coal was the major traffic source on the Norfolk & Western, a fact reflected by the railroad owning more than 40,000 hopper cars (73 percent of its fleet) in the mid-1950s. *Norfolk & Western*

The Pennsylvania Railroad inaugurated its TrucTrain service from Chicago to New York and Philadelphia in 1955. Using new 75-foot flatcars, the service spurred a big upward trend in piggyback traffic in the late 1950s. *Pennsylvania Railroad*

Privately owned cars don't fall under these categories (in the transition era, this included most tank cars and refrigerator cars). They are to be handled as specified by their owners, which usually means returning them to their originating stations when they become empty.

The motivation for railroads to get foreign cars off-line (and to have an adequate supply of their own cars) is *per diem*, the daily rate that a railroad must pay the car owner for having a car on its line. This rate increased over the years, and for our 1955 example, it was $2.40 per car per day. The per diem charge kicked in at midnight, so at terminal cities, railroads worked in the evening to drop cars off on interchange tracks before the clock struck 12 and per diem charges were tallied.

The complete system is a bit more complicated, as it also involves mileage rates for some car types, but the bottom line is that railroads have incentives to keep cars moving and invest in new cars.

Trends

The period from 1940 to 1960 saw tremendous changes in equipment as well as how traffic and specific goods were handled. Freight car production had picked up in the late 1930s after being stagnant through the Great Depression. Railroad traffic was increasing, spurred by World War II and the increased shipping of materials to Great Britain.

Most freight cars of the period could be expected to have a lifespan of 20–30 years, so railroad rosters of 1940 included many cars built in the 1910s and 1920s.

The boxcar remained the dominant freight car type through the period. By 1940, steel boxcars were being built almost exclusively, although there were still plenty of older single-sheathed

wood boxcars in service. The 40-foot steel boxcar was *the* freight car of the period, and it remained the most common car into the 1960s.

By the mid-1950s, however, shippers were looking for more specialized cars. Weight capacity was increasing, and longer boxcars (50-foot) became more common. Boxcars with internal loading devices and cushion underframes appeared, and insulated plug-door cars began taking traffic away from refrigerator cars and standard boxcars.

New automobiles traveled almost exclusively in double-door boxcars into the 1950s, but because of the cumbersome, time-consuming method of loading autos into boxcars, trucks took more auto traffic. One early method to counter this loss was piggybacking auto truck trailers on flatcars. But the solution that brought this traffic back to railroads, although not until the 1960s, was the multilevel auto rack.

Railroad cars in service 1941–1955

Total number of cars in service (private-owner cars in parentheses)

Car type	1941	1946	1950	1955
Boxcars	738,000 (800)	734,200 (1,800)	721,000 (2,900)	782,500 (4,800)
Hoppers*	839,000 (9,200)	880,600 (7,800)	882,300 (7,500)	514,300 (4,200)
Tank cars	150,000 (141,100)	143,200 (134,200)	150,000 (141,600)	159,000 (151,900)
Refrigerator cars	147,200 (125,100)	135,800 (115,100)	127,200 (108,100)	124,800 (105,000)
Flatcars	66,200 (100)	69,700 (200)	68,000 (300)	60,000 (1,100)
Stock cars	58,800 (4,700)	55,400 (2,300)	48,000 (1,600)	38,900 (1,000)
Gondolas*	—	—	—	293,200 (300)
Covered hoppers*	—	—	—	46,700 (3,900)
Other (revenue)	15,200 (800)	11,600 (700)	12,200 (1,000)	31,800 (1,600)

* Hopper car totals through 1950 included gondola and covered hopper cars

The number of covered hoppers grew significantly through the transition era. Into 1940, the few thousand cars in service carried commodities such as cement, carbon black, and phosphate. By the mid-1950s, covered hoppers had increased in size and were hauling feed, fertilizer, and food-grade products such as sugar, flour, and corn starch—products that had previously been hauled in boxcars (by sack or in bulk). The era of the jumbo covered hopper (100-ton), which saw grain moving from boxcars to covered hoppers, began in the 1960s.

Probably the most significant trend was the increase in trailer-on-flatcar (TOFC), or *piggyback*, traffic. Several railroads had dabbled in TOFC from the 1930s into the 1950s, but the formation of the equipment-sharing consortium Trailer Train (TT) in 1955 resulted in a dramatic upturn in piggyback traffic across the country, as 32 railroads became members of Trailer Train by 1960.

The 75-foot piggyback cars built in 1955, and the 85-footers that debuted in 1958, brought a modern look to piggyback service. TOFC carloadings increased from 168,000 in 1955 to 554,000 in 1960.

Refrigerator cars were also evolving. The 40-foot ice-bunker reefer remained the standard car through the 1950s, but fleets of mechanical reefers—from experimental cars in 1949 to production cars a few years later—were expanding, driven largely by the growing frozen-food industry.

Stock car numbers shrunk dramatically, from almost 60,000 cars in 1940 to just 31,000 in 1960. This trend continued through the 1960s as the use of trucks increased and packing houses shifted locations and moved closer to the sources of the animals.

Car size, capacity, and GRL

Freight cars of the era (as now as well) were classified by their weight restrictions. Cars are typically labeled by their approximate or nominal carrying capacity. For the transition era, this was usually 40-ton, 50-ton, 70-ton, and 100-ton cars. This weight can be found in the capacity line stenciled on car sides, in pounds: 80,000, 100,000, 140,000, or 200,000.

However, these numbers are approximations—the true loading capacity varies based on the weight of the car itself and by the car's Gross Rail Load (GRL), which is the maximum weight of the car plus its load allowed on the rails. (More on how this load limit is calculated and stenciled on cars is found in chapter 2.) The GRL for any given car is determined not only by its structure but also by its wheels and trucks: the size of axle and journal, and the corresponding spring package (more on that in chapter 10).

The GRL is the determining factor in whether cars could go on specific routes. For example, a branch line with light rail and low-capacity bridges might allow 50-ton cars but not 70-ton or heavier cars.

A primary goal of improved car designs from the 1930s into the 1940s was to lower car weight. Heavier cars mean more deadweight being hauled in trains and less lading allowed inside the car before hitting a car's GRL. Improved designs resulted in lighter cars (often by several tons), thus increasing a car's load limit while keeping the GRL the same.

By 1940, most cars (including the ubiquitous 40-foot steel boxcar) had a nominal 50-ton capacity, with a GRL of 169,000 pounds. Cars of this GRL were unrestricted for interchange—meaning they could travel anywhere on the rail system. Common GRLs were
- 103,000 pounds for a 30-ton car
- 136,000 pounds for a 40-ton car
- 210,000 pounds for a 70-ton car
- 251,000 pounds for a 100-ton car

These numbers would all be increased by the AAR in the early 1960s.

Some cars continued to be built with lower weight capacities because their lading was less dense or lighter and didn't require heavier capacity. Refrigerator cars and stock cars, for example, were frequently built with a 40-ton capacity through the 1950s.

Quite a few specialty cars with higher capacities (70- and 100-ton) were on the rails by the 1940s, but they began appearing in larger numbers through the 1950s as more routes began allowing heavier cars. Railroads pushed the move toward larger cars, since larger cars meant fewer total cars needed, fewer cars switched, and less tare (dead) weight in trains.

Anatomy of a freight car

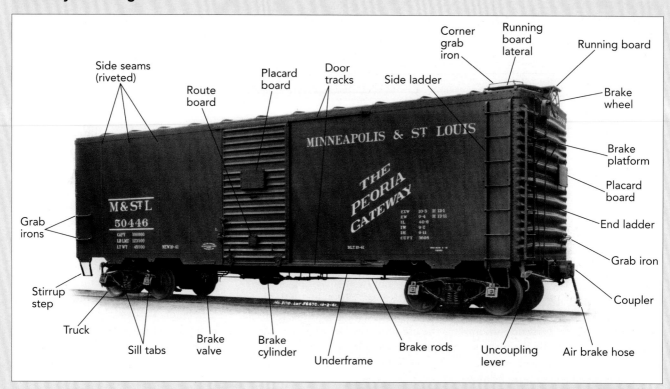

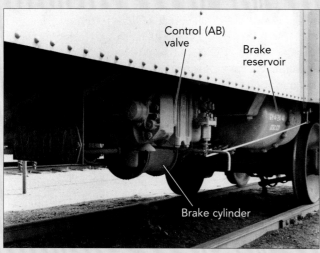

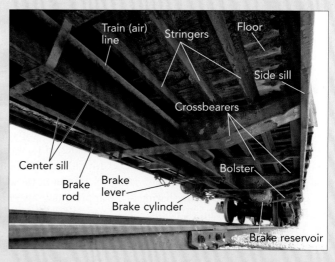

Freight cars have many common components. Knowing what the various parts are called and what they do will help you understand why cars are built the way they are. Many of these details are expanded upon in the car-specific chapters throughout the book.

House cars are the most common car type, and they encompass enclosed cars with sides, ends, and roof. They are boxcars, reefers, and stock cars. The photo at the top of the page shows many components common to these car types.

Grab irons and ladders are located on the car ends and sides at the corners, with drop steps (stirrup steps) at each corner. A ladder (or full-height grabs) is located on the right end of each side. These gave crew members a place to ride when cars were moving, and they allowed access to the roof and a high-mounted brake wheel.

The running board (often incorrectly called a *roofwalk*) is located along the middle of the roof on house cars and covered hoppers, and along the sides and ends of tank cars (flatcars, open hoppers, and gondolas don't have them). Running boards were wood until the early 1940s and then steel after (see chapter 3). The laterals are extensions to the running board that run to the ladder at opposite corners.

Brake gear is common to all cars, but the location of brake components varies by car type. The brake wheel (hand brake) is located at the top of the B end on house cars, hoppers, and gondolas; and it is at deck level on flatcars and tank cars. The brake cylinder, valve, and reservoir are located under house cars and flatcars, found on the end framework of hoppers and covered hoppers, and mounted on the center sill on tank cars. (More on these in chapter 10.)

An air hose at each end connects the train line between cars. At the end of the hose is the metal glad hand—these are placed together and turned to connect them; they separate by themselves when cars are uncoupled. The angle cock—a lever above the hose mounting—allows the air line to be opened or closed.

Each coupler has a knuckle that opens and closes. With knuckles open, cars couple when shoved together, and then the knuckles close automatically and lock. They are uncoupled by using the uncoupling lever, which extends from the coupler to the side of the car at the end. Pulling the lever opens the knuckle on that car. The draft gear is at the rear of the coupler, where its shank (drawbar) connects between the beams of the center sill.

Most cars ride on four-wheel trucks, mounted on the car's bolster at each end. Trucks rotate freely, allowing cars to negotiate curves. (There's more on trucks in chapter 10.)

Steel house cars have route boards and placard boards, which are wood pieces for tacking on notes. Placard boards hold general information notes on lading, handling, and unloading instructions; route boards carry directions on car routing. Placard boards were mounted in high positions into the 1950s and then changed to a lower position. Wood cars didn't have these, as notes could be tacked directly to the car sides.

Tank cars carry a small diamond-shaped placard holder on each end and side that are used to hold standard warning cards when carrying inflammable or hazardous materials.

By the 1930s, new cars were being built on steel underframes of various designs. On house cars and flatcars, these consist of a heavy center sill (a pair of steel beams running the length of the car in the middle), with crossbearers that extend from the center sill to each side and a bolster at the truck location on each end.

Stringers run the length of the car across the crossbearers to support the car floor and sides. A side sill may be used along the ends of the crossbearers, but many house cars did not use them or had small tabs extending downward from the side to cover the ends of the crossbearers and bolster. Car designs of the 1930s and later relied on the carbody itself for strength, which allowed for lighter center sills and framework.

Tank cars, hoppers, and covered hoppers don't have crossbearers or stringers; instead

Cars with cushion underframes, like these Burlington boxcars, have couplers and draft gear that extend outward from the car ends. *J. David Ingles collection*

Brake hoses have metal ends, called *glad hands*, that allow them to be coupled. The rubber gasket provides a tight seal.

Coupler knuckles open outward, allowing automatic coupling. The angle cock, at right, is in the open position.

they rely on a heavier center sill and the carbody for strength and stability.

Cars equipped with cushion underframes have a rubber, spring, or hydraulic mechanism that runs down the center sill between the draft gear at each end. The mechanism absorbs the shock of heavy coupling or slack action. The couplers and draft gear on cars with cushion underframes extend farther from the ends than on standard cars to allow for this movement.

By the end of the 1950s, 70-ton cars could move almost anywhere and 100-ton cars, although still not common, were on the horizon.

Modeling a freight car fleet

What does all this mean in terms of putting together a fleet of cars for a model railroad? Well, first, you'll need to know some specifics of the railroad you model. A Midwestern grain-hauling line will have a dramatically different proportion in types of freight cars than will an Appalachian coal hauler.

A great first step is getting a copy of an *Official Railway Equipment Register*, or ORER, for the period you model. (Check eBay or bookselling sites such as abebooks.com or amazon.com.) Issued quarterly, the ORER lists all the freight cars in service for each railroad and private owner and then breaks down the information by car type and (in most cases) size, capacity, and special equipment.

For example, a look at an April 1955 ORER shows that, at the time, the Minneapolis & St. Louis owned 3,662 freight cars: 2,637 boxcars (all 40-footers and all but 303 were 50-ton cars), 341 hoppers, 339 flatcars, 249 gondolas, 71 covered hoppers (the railroad served cement plants in Iowa), 20 stock cars, and 5 tank cars.

The Rock Island, a larger western (granger) railroad, had 18,821 boxcars, which was about two-thirds of its 30,241 car fleet. The Rock's boxcars included 889 equipped with auto-loading racks and another 235 equipped for carrying auto parts.

Meanwhile, the listing for the Norfolk & Western, a major coal-hauling railroad, showed it owned 56,377 revenue freight cars: 41,190 hoppers (73 percent of its fleet) and 4,174 gondolas compared to just 9,360 boxcars.

Using the ORER, because it breaks cars down by number series and size, makes it easy to determine if that car you found in a photograph is a one-of-a-kind example or part of a large lot of cars.

Lehigh Valley no. 62000 was the first Pullman-Standard PS-1 boxcar built (in 1947). *Lehigh Valley*

Annual travels of a boxcar (Lehigh Valley 62000 in 1954)

Date	Railroad receiving car	Date	Railroad receiving car
1/1	Lehigh Valley	4/20	Union Pacific
1/4	Genesee & Wyoming	5/1	Spokane, Portland & Seattle
1/5	Lehigh Valley	5/1	Great Northern
1/6	New York Central	5/2	Western Pacific
1/6	Niagara Junction	5/3	Atchison, Topeka & Santa Fe
1/8	New York Central	5/21	Belt Ry. of Chicago
1/9	Lehigh Valley	5/21	Chicago South Shore & South Bend
1/12	Genesee & Wyoming		
1/14	Lehigh Valley	5/22	New York Central
1/16	New York, Ontario & Western	5/31	Lehigh Valley
1/17	New York, New Haven & Hartford	6/9	Buffalo Creek
		6/10	Lehigh Valley
1/22	Boston & Maine	6/20	New York, New Haven & Hartford
1/30	Delaware & Hudson		
2/1	Lehigh Valley	6/21	Boston & Maine
2/10	Genesee & Wyoming	7/9	Delaware & Hudson
2/11	Lehigh Valley	7/9	Erie
2/12	Delaware & Hudson	7/10	New York Central
2/13	Boston & Maine	7/24	Niagara Junction
2/19	Delaware & Hudson	7/30	New York Central
2/22	Lehigh Valley	8/1	Chicago River & Indiana
3/3	Genesee & Wyoming	8/5	Chicago, Burlington & Quincy
3/5	Lehigh Valley	8/30	Milwaukee Road
3/6	New York Central	9/24	Indiana Harbor Belt
3/6	Niagara Junction	9/25	Chesapeake & Ohio
3/12	New York Central	9/27	Lehigh Valley
3/15	Indiana Harbor Belt	10/25	Pennsylvania
3/15	Milwaukee Road	10/27	Lehigh Valley
3/17	Union Pacific	11/24	Buffalo Creek
4/9	Southern Pacific	11/26	Lehigh Valley
4/15	Western Pacific	12/21	Wabash
4/19	Spokane, Portland & Seattle	12/23	Union Pacific

It also shows how many cars in a series of older cars are still in service at a certain time.

Your modeled car fleet will also reflect the part of a railroad that you model. If you model a mainline operation—say, the Union Pacific across Nebraska—general freight trains will be heavy on boxcars, with a wide variety of road names, and other car types sprinkled in. That line would also see solid trains of refrigerator cars hauling produce from the West Coast to Chicago and eastern markets. These cars would be mostly Pacific Fruit Express (partially owned by the UP), but some Santa Fe and others would be mixed in. There would also be solid trains of stock cars, especially in fall. Because the cars are coming from and going to destinations not on your layout, you can use almost any car type or road name.

If you model a branch line, your trains should feature cars that serve specific businesses along that line, such as boxcars for grain elevators, tank cars for local fuel distributors, and so on.

Cars that serve specific industries are sometimes "repeaters": a flour mill might get the same Airslide covered hoppers on a regular basis as they shuttle from the mill to a food-processing company and back, or a local cement distributor might see the same two-bay covered hoppers, lettered for the same off-line railroad that serves the cement-producing plant.

If you're freelancing, take a look at a railroad similar to the one you're modeling and use it as a guide for devising the number and type of cars. If you're not sure, a good starting point is to have about half home-road cars, about 25 percent cars from neighboring roads, and the other 25 percent from more distant lines.

The chapters on individual car types should help you determine when various cars appeared in service. For more specific information, see the resources listed on pages 93–95, which provide comprehensive information on rosters and car details. In addition to magazines and books, railroad historical societies and fan groups have online or published information on freight cars.

CHAPTER TWO

Paint and lettering

Most views of early 1940s freight yards do not yield a wide variety of color. What you'll typically find is a sea of dark red and brown freight cars, with a few splashes of color in the form of yellow or orange refrigerator cars, plus some black tank cars and hoppers.

There were certainly exceptions to this, but the standard freight-car color of the period was oxide red, which could be found in many shades, from deep red to brown, with names such as Boxcar Red and Mineral Brown. The color wasn't chosen for aesthetics but for economy and for protecting the cars: it was relatively cheap paint that kept metal surfaces from rusting and wood ones from rotting.

A Chesapeake & Ohio painting crew uses a stencil and spray gun to finish the lettering on a newly rebuilt C&O hopper car in 1955. *Chesapeake & Ohio*

13

Lettering on this new Santa Fe boxcar, built in 1959, includes the usual data, capacity, and reporting marks and number. It also features a large logo, SHOCK CONTROL lettering that calls out the car's cushion underframe, its AAR car class (XML), and the railroad car class (BX-79). *J. David Ingles collection*

This view shows details of a Great Northern boxcar's dimensional data, along with information on special equipment (Miller lubricating pads in the journal boxes), the location of the brake slack-adjustment lever, and dates of maintenance on the sideframe as well as on the end of the brake cylinder (at left). *Great Northern*

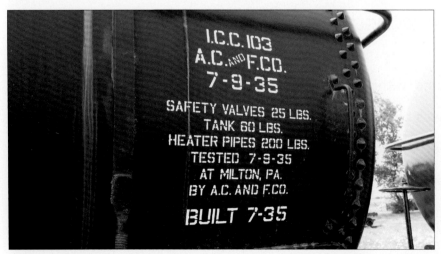

Tank car stenciling includes ICC class (103), car builder (ACF), and the date and location of tank and valve testing.

Refrigerator cars were an exception. Led by the orange of Pacific Fruit Express and yellow of the Santa Fe, Fruit Growers Express, and others, most reefers could easily be picked out of a train by their bright paint schemes. The trade-off was that, especially when steam locomotives were dominant, these cars showed soot and grime rather quickly after painting.

Basic lettering

Into the 1940s, most freight car lettering was rather mundane: reporting marks, car number, capacity data, and, if space allowed, the spelled-out road name possibly with a railroad herald. Lettering was generally white, but it could sometimes be yellow. Colored lettering was used on lighter-colored cars.

Let's take a look at the basic lettering that was required on all cars, along with some specialized lettering, which varied among car types.

Road name and herald. These weren't required, but most railroads spelled out their road names on outside-sheathed (smooth-sided) boxcars and other cars where space allowed. On older single-sheathed wood boxcars, with outside bracing, the road name was often left off.

Slogans and brands. The transition era saw the introduction of many new streamlined passenger trains. Railroads wisely saw freight cars as rolling billboards for their new named trains, and they splashed train names and slogans primarily on boxcars. The better-known examples tended to be the railroads with the largest freight car fleets, which would be seen on trains across the country. Common examples include Santa Fe's *Chief* and *Super Chief,* Burlington's Way of the *Zephyrs,* the Chicago & North Western's *400* Fleet, Seaboard's *Orange Blossom Special,* and Union Pacific's Road of *The Streamliners.*

Privately owned and leased cars often carried the names and brands of their lessees. This was especially true for meat reefers (which were in dedicated service to a specific packing company), as well as for tank cars and covered hoppers owned or leased by petroleum and chemical companies.

Reporting marks and number.
Reporting marks are the unique set of identifying initials assigned to every railroad and private car owner. Private owners (non-railroad) have reporting marks ending in X. Each car's number is unique to that set of reporting marks. The reporting marks and number must also be placed on car ends.

Capacity. This is the car's nominal capacity in pounds. Most transition-era cars were 40-ton (80,000-pound), 50-ton (100,000-pound), or 70-ton (140,000-pound) cars. This capacity was largely determined by the trucks used (explained in chapter 10).

Load limit. This is the maximum weight limit for a car's load. A star next to the load limit indicated that the limit was based on the car's construction and underframe, not the journals and spring package. This number wouldn't be changed if a car's light weight changed. The load limit is based upon the car's weight when empty, which leads us to…

Light weight. This is the car's actual weight when empty. Through the 1950s, for a 50-ton car, the light weight and load limit when added would total 169,000 (the maximum Gross Rail Load, or GRL). For a 40-ton car it was 136,000, for a 70-ton car it was 210,000, and for a 100-ton car it was 251,000.

The word NEW, with a date, placed to the right of the light weight, indicates the weight was taken when the car was built. Cars are periodically reweighed (every 30 months in the 1940s) and also reweighed after repairs or rebuilding. If the reweighing shows a difference (generally 300 pounds or more), the new weight is stenciled in place, and the date and shop initials where this is done are added in place of the NEW stencil. Tank cars didn't require reweighing because their shipping charge was by gallons.

Dimensional data. For boxcars and reefers, this includes the internal and external height, length, and width. Covered hoppers, open hoppers, and many boxcars and reefers include cubic-foot capacity, while tank cars include capacity in gallons.

Bearing repack date. The journal boxes of solid-bearing trucks

End lettering includes reporting marks and number, and it can also include information on car class (X-3), coupler and brake equipment, and wheels (this car has single-wear, wrought-steel wheels). *Standard Oil Co.*

Agents, train crews, and yard workers would often chalk information on cars regarding routing, lading, train numbers, interchange, and track assignments. *Library of Congress*

Many railroads advertised their passenger trains with slogans on freight cars, as shown on this Santa Fe boxcar touting the railroad's *El Capitan* streamliner. Note also the numerous chalk marks. *Library of Congress*

World War II inspired many versions of BUY WAR BONDS lettering. Railroad anniversaries and other events have rated special lettering over the years. *Library of Congress*

The New York Central painted several hundred boxcars in a special scheme for its Pacemaker package service. This car, because it is not intended for interchange, has dimensional data omitted—just reporting marks, number, load limit, and light weight. *J. David Ingles collection*

have bearing pads or cotton waste containing oil to lubricate the bearings (see chapter 10). The dates these were replaced are marked, along with the railroad's or shop initials.

AAR classification. Cars' AAR mechanical classifications (for example, XM for a general-purpose boxcar) began appearing on cars in the 1950s.

Built date. The month and year of a car's construction appear near the dimensional data. A rebuilt car will have both the built date and rebuilt date stenciled on.

Builder's insignia. Car manufacturers often stencil their initials, insignia, or logo on each car side. Cars built by a railroad's own shop usually don't include this.

Routing and loading information. Cars in dedicated service for a specific customer would be stenciled with information as to where the car should be sent when empty, and/or what route to use. Cars used for specific lading (especially tank cars and covered hoppers in dedicated service) are lettered with that information.

Special equipment. Specially equipped cars—such as those with loading racks, cushioned underframes, or a special lining—have lettering or logos to indicate this. Automobile boxcars (with loading racks) have a 3"-wide, horizontal white stripe on the door (the right-hand door on double-door cars) with the car's inside center height stenciled on the stripe and the rack type stenciled below the stripe.

Test information. Tank cars include the date and location where the tank, safety valves, steam lines, and other equipment were tested, along with the relevant data. Tank cars also include the ICC specification class for the car.

Chalk marks. Car agents and others would add chalk notations on cars to indicate routing, train numbers, track numbers, and other special information. The marks would usually be found in the lower corners of the sides or sometimes next to the doors.

Paint scheme evolution

Paint schemes remained rather drab through the 1940s. However, after World War II, as railroads placed more colorful streamlined passenger trains in service, they began expanding their color palettes for freight cars as well.

Railroads used special paint schemes for dedicated-service cars, such as New York Central's red-and-gray Pacemaker boxcars, which served the railroad's less-than-carload (LCL) merchandise service. Other similar cars were operated by Southern Pacific (black, and later silver cars for its Overnite LCL service), Missouri Pacific (blue-and-white), and others.

By the late 1950s, railroads began adopting colorful schemes for general-service cars. These included bright red cars from the Burlington, Great Northern, Minneapolis & St. Louis, and Santa Fe; yellow-and-green cars from Chicago & North Western and Rutland; and red-white-and-blue boxcars from Bangor & Aroostook Interesting patterns were also used, such as Central of Georgia's "blimp" boxcars that featured a huge horizontal silver oval on a black car.

With the era of specialized cars emerging, railroads also began putting information about cushion underframes and loading devices on their cars (such as Santa Fe's Shock Control cars, shown on page 14, and Southern Pacific's Hydra-Cushion underframe cars, shown on page 27).

Tank cars began to perk up as well, with chemical manufacturers in particular adding their own paint schemes and logos to leased and owned cars.

Other trends emerging in the 1950s were the use of reflective paint and the use of decal striping (such as 3M Scotchlite). Although these materials wouldn't be required until later, some railroads began using them to increase nighttime visibility and lower the risk of grade-crossing accidents.

Among the most appealing features of modeling the 1940s and 1950s is the tremendous number of possible road names and paint schemes available to model. There were 129 Class 1 railroads operating in 1955, with hundreds more short lines and private owners. Coupled with the number of car types, this means most modelers have thousands of choices that are appropriate for their given railroad and era.

In 1954, the Central of Georgia painted a batch of 50-foot boxcars in a unique scheme, with a large silver oval surrounded by black. They became known as "blimp" or "football" scheme cars. *J. David Ingles collection*

In 1955, the Chicago & North Western added 4-foot-tall Scotchlite reflective lettering to a new order of PS-1 boxcars, as seen in this staged photo promoting their improved visibility at grade crossings at night. *Chicago & North Western*

Among the most distinctive and colorful schemes of the transition era was displayed by Bangor & Aroostook's sizable fleet of red, white, and blue boxcars with STATE OF MAINE PRODUCTS lettering. *J. David Ingles collection*

17

CHAPTER THREE

Boxcars

A group of new boxcars is on its way to the Union Pacific from Pullman-Standard in 1947. The 40-foot steel boxcar remained the most common car on American freight trains through the 1950s, hauling everything from boxed goods to bulk grain. *C. P. Fox*

The ubiquitous 40-foot boxcar was the standard freight car of the transition era, making up the bulk of most freight trains. Along with general merchandise and products, boxcars were used for dry bulk products such as grain, many chemicals, and even coal and coke.

Boxcars certainly aren't all the same. Height and length variations, double-door cars for auto service, and different details in ends, roofs, doors, and brake gear gave boxcars of the 1940s and '50s tremendous variety in appearance.

In 1940, there were still plenty of wood-sheathed boxcars in service (a few would continue to be built in the 1940s), but almost all new-car construction had shifted to all-steel designs. In addition, railroad shops were rebuilding older wood cars with steel sides and ends to create essentially new cars.

As with other car types, boxcars—whether built by a freight-car manufacturer or by railroad shops—usually followed standard car designs put forth by the American Association of Railroads (AAR) and its predecessor, the American Railway Association (ARA), and—even farther back in time—the United States Railroad Administration (USRA).

Wood-sheathed cars

Among the most common wood-sheathed cars were those built to USRA designs during United States Railroad Administration control of U.S. railroads during World War I and immediately after. Two 40-foot designs were built: a single-sheathed 50-ton car and a double-sheathed 40-ton car. A total of 25,000 of each were built under USRA direction, but the single-sheathed version proved popular enough that railroads through the 1920s ordered thousands of additional cars to the same or very similar designs. Many cars ran through the 1940s and 1950s.

Both cars had steel underframes, but the double-sheathed car (interior and exterior sheathing over a wood frame) had a heavy fishbelly-shaped center sill that was easy to spot. The single-sheathed car didn't require the heavy center sill, as its steel truss-style bracing added strength to the car.

The USRA single-sheathed cars can be spotted by having four panels on each side of the door, diagonals that angle down and outward from the door on three panels, and three-piece Murphy ends with a 5/5/5 pattern (seven corrugations on each panel from top down). Some USRA copies had Murphy 7/8 ends, and many later received steel doors.

Two other common single-sheathed designs that lasted into the transition era were Mather cars and Fowler cars. The Mather Co. built boxcars (as well as reefers and stock cars) to simple designs using common components. Mather single-sheathed cars had three panels on each side of the door with steel braces angling down and out in each panel, a pair of angled straps on each end panel, and wood ends and doors.

This Chicago & North Western boxcar, built in 1925, is a variation of the USRA single-sheathed design. The 40-foot, 50-ton car has Murphy 7/8 ends and a brake wheel on a vertical staff. *Trains magazine collection*

Double-sheathed USRA boxcars had 5/5/5 Murphy ends, straight side sills, and deep fishbelly underframes. These 40-foot, 40-ton cars were often rebuilt with steel sides through the 1940s. *Trains magazine collection*

Mather cars were 40-foot, 40-ton boxcars with wood sides, ends, and roof. Mather cars used common steel structural shapes for side bracing. *Trains magazine collection*

Fowler cars also had wood ends and roofs, wood doors, and three panels on each side of the door. Diagonals were only on the inner panels; the outside panels had angled straps. More than 70,000 Fowlers and clones were built, mainly for Canadian lines as well as

the Chicago & North Western, Rio Grande, and Rock Island.

Many cars that initially looked like Fowlers were also built through the 1930s, but with steel ends, doors, and roof. When identifying single-sheathed cars, look for the number of panels, the

Fowler boxcars and copies, such as this Milwaukee Road car, had wood ends and three panels on each side with diagonal bracing on two panels and angle straps on the end panels. *J. David Ingles collection*

The Pennsy's X-29 boxcar was the first common steel boxcar. The 40-foot car is short, which makes it stand out in trains of later cars. Most had flat steel ends like this one, and the Youngstown door is likely a replacement for the original Creco door. *J. David Ingles collection*

The 1932 ARA boxcar introduced the basic appearance that boxcars would have for the next 25 years. This 9'-3" inside-height car, built for Norfolk Southern in 1935, has 4/4 Dreadnaught ends with square corner posts and tabbed sides, with tabs covering the ends of the bolsters and underframe crossbearers. *Norfolk Southern*

direction of the diagonals, and the type of doors, ends, and roof.

Early steel cars

The move to steel boxcars began in earnest in the 1920s, with the 1923 ARA boxcar. Although not adopted as a standard (it became a "recommended practice" car), the design was widely produced. This 40-foot car was noticeably shorter in height (8'-7" inside height) than later cars. Most had flat riveted ends and three-panel Creco doors, although later cars had Youngstown doors and Dreadnaught corrugated ends.

The Pennsylvania Railroad built about 30,000 cars to this basic design through the 1930s, another 11,000 were built for the Baltimore & Ohio, and 10,000 similar cars built for other railroads. The Pennsy cars in particular were common sights in trains across the country well into the 1950s.

The next significant car design, the 1932 ARA boxcar, receives the credit for starting the movement toward a common appearance that, other than changes in height and some body details, would remain consistent through the 1950s.

The 1932 design was a significant rework of earlier steel cars that fixed problem areas and made them taller and stronger but lighter—3,000 to 4,000 pounds less than earlier, smaller cars.

In the new design, the body shell itself was now responsible for its own strength, unlike earlier designs in which the sides were simply sheathing over heavy bracing.

The redesigned body aided a major change in the underframe: the elimination of the heavy C-channel side sill of earlier cars. The overall underframe was lighter, with side sills eliminated completely, and just a flange holding the bottom of the sides. This resulted in distinctive tabs extending below the sides, which covered the ends of the body bolsters and cross-reinforcing channels on the underframe.

The car sides comprised a series of vertical panels (usually five on each side of the 6-foot sliding door) riveted together on narrow Z-shaped vertical

Aluminum experimental cars

The mid-1940s saw a burst of experimental boxcars being built that used aluminum as the main material for the carbody. These cars were built largely at the behest of the country's major aluminum companies, Alcoa and Reynolds.

Aluminum construction was touted for its light weight (a 40-foot aluminum boxcar saved about 5,400 pounds compared to a steel car), which meant a lower tare weight and higher payload. Other benefits were not needing exterior paint and a lower risk of body corrosion. These experimental cars were built to the AAR standard designs of the day.

The first aluminum boxcar was Great Northern 2500, which was built as an express boxcar in November 1944 at the GN shops using aluminum from Alcoa. In February 1945, 30 additional boxcars followed. They were built by Mount Vernon using Reynolds aluminum: 10 each for Alton (express), Rock Island (express), and Minneapolis & St. Louis (merchandise service). The Chesapeake & Ohio (general service) and Nickel Plate (express) followed in 1947 with 10 homebuilt aluminum cars each (Alcoa).

Alton aluminum boxcar no. 1200 was designed for express service. Note the twin air hoses (brake and signal) and the steam-line pipe below the coupler. *Alton Railroad*

Aluminum boxcars didn't catch on, as railroads felt the higher initial cost was not worth the cars' advantages. However, most cars remained in service through the transition era.

---

posts. The initial inside height was 9'-0"—noticeably taller than the ARA 1923 cars but quite a bit shorter than later AAR cars. An alternate known as the modified 1932 design had a taller body (9'-4").

More than 17,000 cars were built to the 1932 ARA design for 25 railroads through 1942.

Variations

A key to the 1932 and later AAR cars was the number of options allowed in the basic design. Railroads and manufacturers could choose from various brands and styles of individual components, including ends, doors, roofs, trucks, and brake gear.

Ends. The most common end used was the Dreadnaught, made by the Standard Railway Equipment Co. The original design featured a series of large horizontal corrugations across the entire end, with smaller triangular corrugations between the ends of the large corrugations. Variations of this end are still in use.

These ends are made from two or more sections joined at horizontal seams. The height of these sections varied depending upon the height of the car. Describing the variations involves listing the number of

This Western Pacific boxcar, built in 1937, is a 1937 AAR car with 4/5 Dreadnaught ends with the square corner posts that were used until 1940. It has an inside height of 9'-6", which is lower than most 1937 AAR cars. *W. C. Whittaker*

Built in 1941, this Minneapolis & St. Louis car illustrates the rounded corners found on 1937 AAR cars after 1940, the result of the W-section corner post. This car has an inside height of 9'-11". *Pullman-Standard*

Tank boxcar

One notable group of 40-foot boxcars weren't really boxcars. Class XT cars looked like AAR boxcars from the outside, but on the inside, they held cryogenic tanks for carrying compressed gases as liquids. From 1940 through 1961, three companies built about 680 of these cars. Most were leased to Linde/Union Carbide, but Air Reduction Co. (51) and National Cylinder Gas (9) also leased cars.

Early cars (through 1944) were short (9'-5" interior height), while later cars (and all ACF cars) had a 10'-8" height to accommodate larger interior tanks. The cars had small end doors for access to tank safety vents and roof hatches to access vacuum valves. Loading and unloading was done through controls behind the side doors.

These were nominal 70-ton capacity cars, owing to the additional weight of the tanks—the car's light weight was about 118,000 pounds (compared to about 45,000 pounds for a standard 40-foot boxcar).

Although it appears to be a standard 40-foot boxcar, Linde no. 230 houses interior cryogenic tanks for carrying compressed gases as liquids. This boxcar was built in 1942. *J. David Ingles collection*

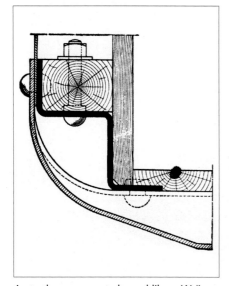

A steel corner post shaped like a W (in heavy black) allows the end (at right) to curve around it to the side to create a stronger assembly. *Standard Railway Equipment Co.*

New York Central no. 164000, built in 1947, is a 1944 AAR design. The 10'-6" inside-height car has 4/4 improved Dreadnaught ends, a panel roof, and Youngstown doors. *New York Central*

corrugations on each section. On the 1932 car, a 4-over-4 pattern (written as a 4/4 Dreadnaught) was used on all but one Dreadnaught order, which used a 4/5 pattern.

Other ends included the older Murphy design (as on the USRA cars), used on 1,800 cars; a flat riveted end, used on 2,650 cars; and the Buckeye, which has a series of wide horizontal corrugations, used on 500 Erie cars.

Roofs. The most common roof was the raised panel, a new design

for this car. The panel roof would become the most common house-car roof through the 1950s. These are made from a series of separate sections or panels, connected at raised seams by an inverted-U-shaped seam cap. Each panel has a rectangular raised section for strength, so no subroof or framework is needed.

Some 1932 ARA cars (about 4,500) had older lap-seam roofs. These lacked the raised panels and had sections joined at flat seams. Another 1,000 cars

had Viking roofs, which had a series of corrugations parallel to the roof seams. About 700 Canadian Pacific and 500 Nickel Plate Road cars had radial roofs, which featured a raised-seam design with a curved profile.

Doors. Most 1932 ARA cars were equipped with Youngstown doors, which would become the most common sliding door through the 1950s. About 1,800 received three-panel Creco doors, the same style as used on most 1923 ARA cars.

Brake gear. Several companies made brake wheels and brake gear for these and later cars. Each manufacturer had a distinctive brake wheel design (see chapter 10). Just over 2,000 cars received brake wheels on vertical staffs, the last such cars delivered.

Underframes. About 1,300 of these cars received Duryea cushioned underframes. These had an enclosed center sill that was spring loaded, which was designed to cushion the carbody from shocks in switching and slack action. The primary spotting feature is extended draft gear, which protrudes from the car ends more than from a standard car.

The 1937 AAR boxcar

Boxcar evolution through the next two decades was largely a matter of increasing height and width, along with refining designs for individual car components. The next official design revision was the 1937 AAR boxcar, which saw an increase in interior height to 10'-0", with taller modified options at 10'-4" and 10'-6".

The number of component variations dropped compared to the 1932 car, but there remained many deviations from the standard. Most 1937 cars received panel roofs and Dreadnaught ends. The standard cars had 4/5 Dreadnaught ends, while the modified versions had 5/5 ends. Some cars received Buckeye or Deco (a waffle pattern) ends, and some were equipped with Viking roofs.

The standard door opening was still 6 feet, but many cars were built with 7- and 8-foot openings. Youngstown corrugated doors remained the most common door type, but Superior panel doors were applied to many 1937 cars.

Another distinction in spotting these cars is at the corners between the ends and sides. Through 1940, cars had square corner posts, so there was a sharp angle where the end met the side. A design revision replaced the square post with a W-section post, with the end wrapping around the outside legs of the W in a curve. The Dreadnaught ends became rounded where they met the sides at the post.

This Missouri-Kansas-Texas car, built by ACF in 1950, is a 1944 AAR car with ACF proprietary ends and a diagonal-panel roof, which began appearing in 1948. *ACF*

Built in 1949, Grand Trunk Western no. 515668 illustrates the improved Dreadnaught ends found after 1948, with a horizontal rectangular corrugation at the top. The car has a seven-panel Superior door. *ACF*

Early 1937-design cars had square posts; cars built after 1940 (and successive AAR designs) had W corner posts. A 1940 ad from the Standard Railway Equipment Co. (maker of Dreadnaught ends) declared that the new ends were 25 percent stronger than the older-style square posts.

Through the 1930s, most running boards on house cars were wood, with three parallel 6"-wide planks running the length of the roof (with a gap between boards to allow for drainage). Initially, using wood was cheap, but it required frequent repair; wood could also become slippery in inclement weather.

Metal running boards offered much better traction and durability. They began to appear in the late 1930s, and became mandatory on new equipment as of 1947 (the initial 1944 date was extended).

Metal running boards were available from several manufacturers, with the most common being Apex, Blaw-Knox, Kerrigan, Morton, and U.S. Gypsum. Each varied slightly in design. Apex Tri-lok (the most common), Blaw-Knox, and Kerrigan have a lengthwise rectangular pattern. U.S. Gypsum boards through 1954 have a stretched honeycomb-style pattern; after that,

By the time this car rolled out of Burlington's Havelock, Neb., shops in 1958, the era of the 40-foot, 6-foot-door boxcar was closing. The car has a five-panel Superior door with lowered tack boards. Note the L near the door. *Chicago, Burlington & Quincy*

Combination plug/standard doors, as on this 1956 Great Northern car, became popular in the mid-1950s. Note the straight side sill on this homebuilt car.
Great Northern

This Northern Pacific car, built in 1948, looks like a standard AAR 40-foot car, but it has a continuous sill sheet from bolster to bolster instead of standard sill tabs.
J. David Ingles collection

they became rectangular. Morton's were pressed steel with perforated holes.

The 1937 AAR design proved extremely popular. It was the most common AAR-design boxcar, with more than 40,000, including variations, built through 1947.

The 1944 AAR boxcar

The next design upgrade came with the 1944 AAR car. The most common height was 10'-6", although some were built at 10'-0". Among the key spotting features are an updated end, known as the improved Dreadnaught end. On these ends, long, narrow corrugations between the wide corrugations replaced the small triangular "darts" of the original end. The taller cars had 4/4 improved ends; the 10'-0" cars had 3/4 improved ends. The appearance changed slightly in 1948 with the addition of an additional thin rectangular horizontal corrugation above the standard corrugations.

A variation that appeared on some cars beginning around 1950 was the elimination of the narrow corrugations, leaving only the wide corrugations. This version—the modified improved Dreadnaught—has been termed the "dartnaught" end by some modelers.

A proprietary end produced by American Car & Foundry (ACF) in the late 1940s was another variation. Applied to 2,550 cars from 1948 to 1950, the ACF end had large horizontal corrugations that were wide in the middle and tapered to a narrower profile at each end.

Youngstown doors remained the most popular, although Superior doors were also used on many cars. Variations in the Youngstown door include the number of corrugations on each panel, with (from top) 5/7/5, 4/5/4, and 3/5/5 patterns.

Superior doors have five or seven panels. Early doors (through 1949) had seven evenly-spaced panels; later doors had uneven spacing, with the third panel from top wider to accommodate the large placard board. Five-panel doors began appearing in 1952. Six-foot door openings remained the most common through the 1940s, but 7- and 8-foot openings (and even 9-footers) became more common into the 1950s.

Ladders are another spotting feature. Count the rungs: ladders with seven or eight rungs can be found. (The Burlington car on the opposite page has an eight-rung ladder.)

The panel roof remained the standard until about 1948, when an improved version appeared, the diagonal panel. As photos show, the raised portions in each section are angled across the panel, replacing the rectangular raised areas of the standard panel. Roofs in both styles were installed through the mid-1950s.

Welded construction became more common into the 1950s. On welded cars, a thin vertical weld seam appears between side panels instead of the seam line with rivets.

Production of 40-foot boxcars slowed considerably in the 1950s, as railroads and customers began moving toward 50-foot cars and specially equipped cars.

Pullman's PS-1

Pullman-Standard built thousands of ARA and AAR boxcars through the mid-1940s. In 1947, P-S began producing its PS-1 line of boxcars. The car was basically an AAR 1944 design but with Pullman-Standard's proprietary design ends, roof, underframe (after 1949), and optional doors.

The ends provide probably the best overall spotting feature. The PS-1 end has a series of wide corrugations without the in-between small darts or narrow corrugations of the Dreadnaught end. The PS-1

Pullman's PS-1 cars can be identified by their welded construction and unique ends, which have a series of rounded corrugations. This car, built in 1957, has P-S doors with raised panels. *Pullman-Standard*

This Rutland PS-1 boxcar has a 7-foot-wide Superior five-panel door. Many chalk marks can be seen on the car. *J. David Ingles collection*

Automobile boxcars have two sliding side doors. Some, like this single-sheathed, 50-foot Northern Pacific car, have swinging doors on the A (non-brake) end for end-loading vehicles. *E. G. Boyd, collection of Jay Williams/Big Four Graphics*

Through the 1940s and '50s, auto boxcars were identified by a white stripe on the right-hand door. This 50-foot Pere Marquette car also has stenciling indicating that it should be returned to the C&O at Flint, Mich., when empty. *J. David Ingles collection*

This 1930s view shows the labor-intensive process of loading autos. An automobile is elevated in the Evans rack at right, above the one being blocked in place on the floor. *Library of Congress*

Evans auto racks were fairly simple devices that allowed an auto in each end of the boxcar to be elevated, allowing another auto to be placed on the floor in each end. Racks could be stowed at ceiling level when not in use. *Evans Products Co.*

corrugations are slightly wider at the outside ends and narrower in the middle. From 1949 onward, the ends have a series of small rectangular protrusions above the top corrugation.

The PS-1 roof is similar to the panel roof, but the raised sections are wider at the outside and get narrower at the roof peak. This is sometimes described as a "bow-tie" appearance. Originally the end roof panels were plain (flat) with no raised area. After 1949, all panels had bow-tie protrusions.

Youngstown and Superior doors are common on PS-1s, but Pullman's own design doors were installed on some cars. The PS-1 door has five panels, similar to a Superior, but each panel has a raised rectangular corrugation. Six- and 8-foot doors were the most common, but cars were built with 7- and 9-foot doors as well.

A feature in Pullman-Standard's sales pitch was welded construction, although some early PS-1s featured riveted construction. The PS-1 was built in 40- and 50-foot lengths. Along with the earlier detail variations, other spotting features include the type of trucks, running boards, and brake wheels. Many double-door 50-foot cars were built, and by the late 1950s, 50-footers were built with plug doors (insulated cars) and combination plug/sliding doors.

The PS-1 proved immensely popular. Through 1959, about 75,000 40-foot PS-1s were built for 79 railroads and private owners. A total of 22 railroads owned at least 1,000 PS-1s, with five railroads owning at least 5,000 (Chicago & North Western, Louisville & Nashville, New York Central, Rock Island, and Southern). In addition, another 20,000 50-foot PS-1s were built prior to 1960.

Double-door and auto boxcars

Into the 1950s, the most common way of carrying new automobiles to market was in boxcars. Although not an efficient method in terms of tare weight and ease of loading and unloading, this was the best railroads could do until development of the 85-foot (and later, 89-foot) auto rack cars around 1960.

Ventilated boxcars

Ventilated boxcars were largely used by railroads in the Southeast. They were also known as *melon* or *watermelon* cars, named for common lading. These cars were equipped with two sliding doors: one solid and one screened. The car ends were equipped with vents. In ventilator service, this allowed air to flow through the car, much like a refrigerator car in ventilator service. Ventilated boxcars could be used as standard boxcars by closing the end vents and using solid doors over the door openings.

Ventilated boxcars were popular in the steam era, but by the 1940s, ventilated reefers assumed much of their traffic. Plenty continued in service through the transition era. As of 1942, the Atlantic Coast Line (ACL), Seaboard Air Line, and Central of Georgia railroads each had more than 3,000 in service, and the Louisville & Nashville

Ventilated boxcars had vents on the ends and pairs of doors on each side—one screened, one solid—to allow airflow through the car during transit. *Seaboard Air Line*

had 2,000. Other operators included Chesapeake & Ohio, Norfolk & Western, Southern, Florida East Coast, and Charleston & Western Carolina (an ACL subsidiary).

Although almost all auto boxcars had double doors, not all double-door boxcars were built specifically for auto service. They also carried furniture, appliances, auto parts, and other bulky items.

Auto boxcars were built in 40- and 50-foot versions. They followed the same basic construction and details as contemporary AAR-design cars, as builders took their existing designs and fitted them with double side doors to allow loading. Most were all-steel cars by 1940 (and many railroads rebuilt earlier wood boxcars into steel-sided auto cars in the late 1930s into the 1940s). Some 40-foot auto cars were built through the 1940s, but by 1950, the move had shifted to 50-foot versions to accommodate larger automobiles.

Some auto cars were equipped with end doors on the A end to facilitate loading and unloading, but most automobiles were loaded and unloaded through the side doors—the end doors were more often used for trucks and other large equipment. This necessitated a wide door opening, so most auto cars had a pair of side doors with a 16-foot-wide opening (although some, especially early boxcars, were narrower, at 12'-6").

Auto boxcars were often in pool service, assigned to a particular plant. Railroads would own cars proportionate to their length of hauls on various routes. Cars would often be stenciled with return instructions, as

This Southern Pacific 50-foot car with a hydraulic cushion underframe, built in 1957, represents the trend boxcars were taking by the late 1950s. The car has an 8-foot door opening and straight side sill. *J. David Ingles collection*

seen on the Pere Marquette car on the opposite page.

As door openings varied, so did doors: Some had pairs of same-width doors (two 8-footers for a 16-foot opening), but others had varying sizes, such as 8- and 6-foot doors for a 14-foot opening. A variation that became common toward the mid- and late 1950s was the double-door car with one plug door and one standard door.

The large opening took away some of the strength of the side, so double-door cars had reinforcing strips along the side sills below the doors, often extending the full car length. These strips could be straight or tapered depending upon the manufacturer.

Auto loading

Floor racks or restraints were used to hold automobiles in position when loaded. A standard boxcar could hold two autos: one in each end of the car. To double capacity, most auto boxcars were equipped with internal racks that allowed an auto in each end to be elevated toward the roof, so another auto could be stored on the floor under each rack. The most popular of these racks was built by Evans.

Cars in auto service were usually stenciled with AUTOMOBILE on each side. To more easily identify cars with racks, in 1939, the AAR adopted a standard for marking boxcars equipped with automobile racks. Auto rack cars received a 3"-wide horizontal white stripe just below center on the right-hand sliding door on each side. In the middle of this stripe was 2"-tall lettering that indicated the car's interior height at the center of the car. Below the stripe was an additional

Built in 1957, this double-door Northern Pacific car has a fishbelly side sill. Railroads advertised their passenger trains on their freight cars through the 1950s, as seen here with ROUTE OF THE VISTA-DOME NORTH COAST LIMITED. *J. David Ingles collection*

General American built more than 500 50-foot cars for its lease fleet in 1950. The cars had 8-foot-wide doors, straight side sills, and Duryea cushioned underframes. *J. David Ingles collection*

stencil showing the number of floor tubes (tie-downs) and the type of rack. In addition, the AAR mechanical code could be stenciled on the car side (XAR for a car with racks).

As boxcars were phased out of auto service, they would have their racks removed (or stowed at ceiling height) and their auto markings and stencils painted out. Since the racks could be stowed at ceiling height (or completely removed rather easily), boxcars would sometimes be pulled in and out of auto service. During World War II, most auto cars (other than those hauling military vehicles) were placed in general service with their racks removed or stowed. Following the war, they were placed back in auto service.

50-foot boxcars

Prior to World War II, most 50-foot boxcars were used for automobiles, furniture, and other specialty service. After the war, the 40-foot boxcar remained the most-popular general-service car. The AAR adopted a standard 50-foot, single-door car in 1942, largely following contemporary 40-foot cars, with a 10'-6" inside height, panel roof, Dreadnaught ends, and 6-, 7-, or 8-foot doors. The design used 16 side panels (compared to 10 for a 40-foot car).

The AAR design had tabs over the ends of the stub sills, in the same manner as 40-foot cars, but a common variation among 50-foot cars was a straight side sill skirt in place of the tabs. This straight skirt could extend

the length of the car or from bolster to bolster. Another variation that became common by the late 1950s was a tapered fishbelly side sill skirt that grew deeper under the door and then angled up to end above the truck bolster.

The number of 50-foot, single-door cars began to grow in the 1950s. Notable was General American's lease fleet of 500-plus cars built in 1950. These cars, with GAEX reporting marks, could be found across the country. They had 8-foot doors, straight side sills, and diagonal-panel roofs, and they were also equipped with Duryea cushioned underframes. Most had Evans loading devices and sported DF (for *damage free*) or NO DAMAGE lettering.

General American, ACF, Pullman, and other builders (along with railroad shops) built various styles of 50-foot cars through the 1950s. Along with the sill variations, their spotting features are similar to 40-foot cars, including ends (rib pattern), doors (width and type: Youngstown or Superior), brake gear, trucks, running boards, sides (number of panels and welded or riveted), and roofs.

By the late 1950s, 50-foot cars of various styles outnumbered 40-foot cars in production.

Insulated boxcars

Starting in the early 1950s, the introduction of the plug door and improvements in insulation brought a growth in fleets of insulated boxcars. Although some 40-foot insulated cars were built, most railroads followed the trend of using 50-foot boxcars.

By the 1950s, fiberglass and then foam (polystyrene and later polyurethane) came into wide use as insulation materials. They were easy to apply between the interior and exterior walls of a freight car, and a thin layer of foam offered a higher insulation value than thick layers of the previously used materials.

Insulated boxcars were equipped with plug doors, which were initially used on refrigerator cars beginning around 1949. When opened, plug doors slide to the side of the openings on tracks, but when maneuvered back to the opening, they insert firmly into the opening with a solid seal. Plug doors allowed wider openings than swinging doors, which was an important feature when using forklifts and loading equipment.

These cars proved to be an immediate success. Tests showed that if the lading was precooled, a foam- or fiberglass-insulated plug-door car would hold the load within a few degrees of the initial temperature over several days in transit.

Insulated boxcars received the AAR code XI, although by the late 1950s, many were classified as bunkerless refrigerated cars, or beverage cars, with an RB or RBL code (the L suffix indicated adjustable bulkheads or other load-restraint equipment).

Insulated boxcars became popular for shipping canned goods and other products that required a clean interior and protection from extreme heat or cold. These cars also began carrying many types of perishables that once required refrigerated transportation.

Among the first insulated boxcars were those built in 1953, when the Bangor & Aroostook and New Haven railroads ordered 550 40-foot insulated cars from Pacific Car & Foundry. Carrying potatoes and newsprint, these cars sported a distinctive red, white, and blue "State of Maine" paint scheme. Fruit Growers Express acquired its first RBL cars in 1954, 40-footers, and other railroads and private owners soon followed.

Other designs and variations

Many railroads built their own freight cars, sometimes following AAR standards and sometimes using their own unique designs.

Among the largest fleet of custom cars was the Milwaukee Road's fleet of welded ribbed-side boxcars. These distinctive cars can easily be spotted by their prominent horizontal corrugations on each side of the door.

The first of these cars began appearing from the railroad's Milwaukee shops in 1937, and by the end of the 1940s, about 13,000 (including 2,000 50-footers) were on the rails.

Advances in insulation materials led to a growing number of insulated boxcars (technically, bunkerless reefers) by the late 1950s. This Burlington car, built in 1958, has an 8-foot plug door and straight side sills. *J. David Ingles collection*

AAR car codes for boxcars		
Class X (Boxcar types*)		
XM	General-service boxcar	
XA	Automobile boxcar, inside height 10 feet or more	
XAB	Automobile boxcar, inside height less than 10 feet	
XAP	Automobile parts car with permanent interior racks	
XAR	Automobile boxcar with auto stowing equipment	
XAF	Automobile or furniture car	
XF	Furniture car (usually larger than a general-service car)	
XI	Insulated boxcar	
XT	Tank boxcar (boxcar with one or more interior tanks)	
Insulated boxcars (classified with refrigerator cars)		
RB	Bunkerless (insulated) car	
RBL	Bunkerless car with loading devices	
Ventilated boxcars*		
VA	Ventilated boxcar for fruits and vegetables	
VM	Ventilated boxcar, partially insulated	
VS	Ventilated boxcar, insulated with swinging side doors	
* H suffix indicates heating equipment		

These boxcars featured several variations including the length of the ribs. Early cars had ribs extending to the car ends, while ribs on later cars stopped short of the ladders and grab irons, with a blank area at the end of each side. Many of the boxcars were equipped with unusual Murphy double-panel welded roofs with two raised sections per panel. Doors included Youngstown, Superior, Creco, and Camel. Car ends were mostly Dreadnaught, and many ends had small inspection/lumber doors.

Another classic design that became a signature for a railroad was Baltimore & Ohio's homebuilt wagon-top boxcars. These unique cars had vertical side panels that wrapped in a curve at the top of the side to become the roof. External vertical channels covered the seams between panels.

Using this design, the B&O rebuilt older cars through the mid-1930s. The railroad then built several series of new 40-foot cars to this design starting in 1937, with a total of 3,000 cars through 1941. These B&O

Baltimore & Ohio's round-roof boxcars were hard to miss. They could be spotted in trains across the country through the 1950s. This 40-foot car was built in 1941.
J. David Ingles collection

The Milwaukee Road built a substantial fleet of 40-foot welded boxcars in the 1930s and '40s. The cars can be spotted by their distinctive horizontal side ribs.
Trains magazine collection

cars had flat slab ends and doors. The rebuilt cars can be identified by their recessed side sills and fishbelly underframes.

The Pennsylvania Railroad also had a fleet of round-roof cars built in the 1930s. Unlike the B&O cars, the roofs on the Pennsy's cars were separate assemblies that fit over the sides and ends. Early cars had a "step" where the roof met the side; these became flush in later construction. The sides of these cars followed conventional steel construction with vertical riveted panels, and the ends for the most part were Dreadnaught.

These cars were class X31 on the PRR, and about 10,000 were built in several series from 1933 to 1936, including single- and double-door

cars. In addition, the PRR had another 2,000 50-foot cars (class X32 and X33). Many of these 40- and 50-foot cars were in auto service. (You can see one of these cars rebuilt as a stock car on page 83.)

The Norfolk & Western and Virginian both had 50-foot cars following the PRR design, and the Detroit, Toledo & Ironton had 40-foot as well as 50-foot round-roof cars.

Seaboard Air Line owned yet another group of round-roof cars. These 1,700 40-foot, single- and double-door cars were built by Pullman-Standard (which coined the "turtle back" name) from 1940 to 1942. These cars had PS ends and AAR underframes, with riveted sides and tabbed sills.

War-emergency boxcars

Although freight car production slowed considerably during World War II, some cars were still built. Steel was in short supply for railroad cars, so railroads and builders were required to use wood in place of steel wherever possible, and the AAR developed several composite war-emergency designs.

The resulting boxcars (like the 1944 Northern Pacific car on the opposite page) featured a steel underframe with standard steel ends and roof, but with a single-sheathed wood body. Railroads receiving similar cars were the Alton, Central of Georgia, Chicago & North Western, Georgia, Nickel Plate, and Wabash. The Santa Fe had the only war-emergency 50-footers.

Rebuilt boxcars

Along with buying and building new cars, railroads from the 1930s through the 1940s rebuilt older boxcars, especially 40-foot, wood-body, steel-underframe cars. By reusing an older car's underframe, adding new steel sides, roof, and ends (if needed), and upgrading the brake gear and trucks, a railroad could have what amounted to a new car for less than the price of an all-new car.

Among the top candidates for rebuilding were the USRA (and clone) single- and double-sheathed boxcars built in 1918 and later. The double-sheathed wood cars in particular were prime candidates for rebuilding. Moisture tended to get trapped between their walls, which made the wood bodies rot and decay faster than those of single-sheathed cars. The heavy underframes of these cars, meanwhile, were quite solid—overbuilt, in fact—and provided a solid base for a rebuilt car.

Several spotting features set these rebuilds apart from ARA and AAR 40-foot cars. Most rebuilt cars kept their original Murphy ends, with distinct narrow corrugations unlike Dreadnaught ends. Cars rebuilt from double-sheathed USRA boxcars retained their underframes with heavy fishbelly center sills, which are clearly visible beneath the car. These cars also had recessed side sills along the bottom of each side, with the side resting on brackets attached to the side sill.

Many rebuilds retained their original interior heights, starting at 8'-10", but some were rebuilt at 10'-4" or 10'-6". This was done either by adding additional material between the original end panels or by giving the cars new ends. While original roofs were sometimes reused, new roofs were often added.

Express boxcars

Express boxcars carried parcels for Railway Express Agency and the U.S. Mail—shipments that garnered a premium price for faster delivery. To provide this service, express traffic was carried at the head end of passenger trains (hence the term *head-end traffic*). Usually this was in standard railroad baggage cars (generally labeled RAILWAY EXPRESS AGENCY), which carried far more mail and express than passenger baggage, but many railroads equipped boxcars for this service as well.

Express boxcars were given AAR code BX (box-express). They were based on contemporary ARA and AAR cars, but required more specialized equipment than their merchandise-car counterparts. Some were rebuilt from older cars for the service, and others were ordered new.

Because they operated in passenger trains at passenger-train speeds (often in excess of 80 mph), they required high-speed trucks. Common trucks included GSC Commonwealth (which looked like a shorter version of a conventional passenger-car truck), Allied Full Cushion (banned after 1955), Chrysler, and Symington-Gould XL (more on trucks in chapter 10).

Express cars were also equipped with steam and train-signal lines and connections. They can be spotted by the pair of air hoses at each end (one for brakes and one for signals) and the pipe connector for steam (see the Alton car on page 21).

Express boxcars sometimes wore special paint schemes to match the colors of a railroad's passenger

A shortage of steel during World War II led to the war-emergency, single-sheathed, wood boxcar design. This Northern Pacific car was built in 1944 and had an interior height of 10'-5". *J. David Ingles collection*

Many railroads rebuilt older wood boxcars. This Omaha Road car was rebuilt from an old USRA double-sheathed car. Note the reused extended Murphy ends and deep fishbelly underframe. *Collection of Jay Williams/Big Four Graphics*

The Union Pacific built this class BX-50-31 express boxcar in 1941. The 40-foot double-door car is short (8'-6" inside height) and is equipped with steam and signal lines. *J. David Ingles collection*

equipment. Many other cars wore basic Pullman green paint to match that of conventional baggage cars. Lettering varied by railroad, but it was often basic, with the railroad name and car number and sometimes RAILWAY EXPRESS AGENCY, EXPRESS, or U.S. MAIL lettering.

Because they did not carry heavy loads, express boxcars often had a light capacity (the UP car shown above is a 25-ton car).

CHAPTER FOUR

Refrigerator cars

Through the 1940s and 1950s, solid trains of refrigerator cars would haul produce from harvest areas to major markets. Here, a Union Pacific train with a long string of orange Pacific Fruit Express reefers makes its way eastward. *Linn H. Westcott*

The ice-bunker refrigerator car (*reefer*, for short) was a staple car of the transition era. Reefers, often in solid trains, carried fruits, vegetables, and meat year-round from growing regions or processing plants to markets. Most ice-bunker cars had a nominal capacity of 30 or 40 tons, which was less than the 50-ton capacity of most boxcars. A reefer fully loaded with produce would rarely approach that weight limit, so there was no need for higher capacity.

In addition, refrigerator cars were often used to haul boxed food, canned goods, and beverages that, although they didn't require refrigeration, needed to be kept from extremes in heat and cold. This traffic migrated to insulated boxcars when those cars became efficient and available in large numbers from the late 1950s into the 1960s.

In the United States, most refrigerator cars were controlled by private owners, not railroads. For example, in 1941, private owners operated 125,000 of the 147,000 reefers in service. This arrangement dates to the mid-1800s, when railroads were reluctant to invest in specialized (expensive) cars that were limited—by season or lading—in what they could haul.

The largest owners during the transition era were Pacific Fruit Express (PFE), owned jointly by Southern Pacific and Union Pacific; Santa Fe Refrigerator Department (SFRD), owned by the Atchison, Topeka & Santa Fe; and Fruit Growers Express (FGE), owned by a large group of eastern railroads. The chart on page 35 lists major owners of refrigerator cars during the 1940s and 1950s.

Many variations of refrigerator cars operated during this time. In the 1920s, a wood-body, steel-underframe refrigerator car was designed by the United States Railroad Administration (USRA) and characterized by a deep fishbelly center sill as on USRA double-sheathed boxcars. Although none were built under USRA direction,

One common wood reefer design was the Mather car, distinguished by its vertical wood sheathing over C-channel side sills. Older Mather cars had wood ends, while modernized cars had Dreadnaught steel ends. This one, leased to Morrell, was built in 1949. *Bill Raia collection*

many similar cars were built to that design. The American Railway Association (ARA) and American Association of Railroads (AAR) did not develop standardized designs for refrigerator cars as they did with boxcars and other freight cars. This resulted in a wide variety of designs of both wood and steel cars through the end of the ice-bunker car era.

Ice-bunker cars

Ice-bunker cars remained the standard for refrigerator service through the 1950s. These cars were relatively inexpensive to build, and the system of icing cars worked well. Ice cars were largely foolproof (a compressor can't fail on a bunker filled with ice), and cars held their temperature well. The biggest challenge—and one that took significant time, resources, and

manpower—was the process of making and storing ice and re-icing cars that was accomplished at icing docks throughout the country.

The cutaway drawing of an ice-bunker car shows how these cars were built and how they work. By 1940, most new refrigerator cars were nominally 40 feet long. However, because of the thick insulation required in the side walls, roof, and floor, as well as the space occupied by the ice bunkers at each end (about 3 feet of car length for each bunker), interior space was much less than in a contemporary 40-foot boxcar. Typical reefer interiors measured about 33 feet long, just over 8 feet wide (compared to 9'-2" for a boxcar), and 7 feet high (10'-0" for a boxcar).

Ice bunkers were located at each end of the car, with a pair of roof hatches above each bunker for loading ice

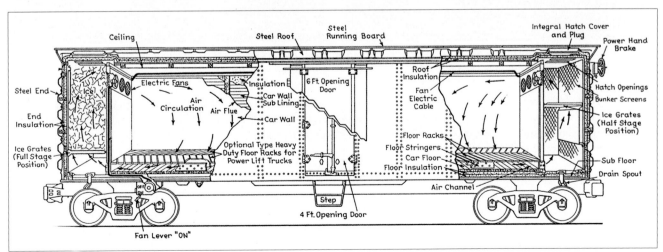

This cutaway drawing of an ice-bunker refrigerator car shows how circulating air cooled the car. *Preco, Inc.*

A worker loads crates of oranges into a reefer. You can see the ice through the grates in the bunker wall above the orange cases. *Library of Congress*

Workers ice a string of reefers on the Santa Fe around 1940. They slide blocks of ice to the tops of refrigerator cars and then chop it as it goes through the hatches into the bunkers. *Library of Congress*

Cars with collapsible bunkers have bunker walls that swing out of the way when the car is not in ice service. *ACF*

Meat reefers have rails at ceiling level to allow sides of meat to hang from steel hooks. *New York Central*

chunks. A grate at the bottom of the bunker allowed water to drain (drains were located at each corner of the car), and another grate at the top of the interior wall allowed cold air to flow from the bunker to the car interior. A typical initial load for a 40-foot car was 9,000–11,000 pounds of ice.

Reefers have interior floor racks that look like pallets. These elevate the load and allow cold air to circulate at floor level. Later reefers also had flues in the side walls for improved air flow.

By 1940, most "modern" ice cars allowed stage icing. In this process, a grate was lowered halfway down the bunker, so a half load of ice was carried in a high position, which provided better cooling than having a half load of ice remaining at the bottom of the bunker.

Also by the transition era, many new cars were equipped with collapsible bunkers, with walls that could be folded out of the way to provide more floor space if the car was carrying lading that didn't require icing.

Almost all produce cars could also be used in ventilator service. This involved propping open the ice hatches to allow outside air to flow through the car while it was in motion. Depending upon the outside temperature, this was often enough to cool products such as potatoes, onions, and bananas without the need for ice.

Interior, air-circulating fans appeared in 1941. These were located high on the wall between the bunker and car interior and forced cool air into the interior. Early fans were mechanically powered (direct-drive) by a rubber wheel that could be placed in contact with one of the car's wheels. Later fans were electric and powered by small generators turned by a car's wheel.

Until 1950, refrigerator cars had pairs of swinging side doors, usually with 4-foot-wide openings. Door height varied among cars. A latch bar on the right-hand door sealed the doors, with a handle crossing to the left door. Sliding plug doors arrived in 1950.

Most exterior refrigerator car components, such as ends, sides, and roofs, paralleled contemporary boxcar design and construction. Some wood reefers were still being built with wood roofs (actually a sandwich of multiple layers of wood and metal) long after boxcars had switched to steel, but by 1940, most new cars received steel panel roofs. Dreadnaught ends were most common on steel cars, albeit shorter than on boxcars, with fewer corrugations on each panel. Many wood cars retained their wood ends through the 1950s.

Produce and meat cars

Refrigerator cars were generally built to carry either produce (fruits, vegetables, and canned goods/beverages) or meat. Produce cars (AAR class RS) had ice bunkers and roof hatches that could be set for ventilator service.

Meat reefers were also similar, but they were also equipped with meat rails—beams that extended along the interior ceiling, so sides of beef could be hung on hooks for transit.

In place of ice bunkers in each end, most meat reefers (about 60 percent) were equipped with brine tanks. Filled with a combination of crushed ice and salt, the brine tanks would hold the mix until they were emptied. This feature wasn't apparent from the

Refrigerator car ownership		
The major owners of ice-bunker refrigerator cars in 1940 and 1954		
Produce and meat reefers		
Owner	1940	1954
ART	13,000	9,100
BREX**	2,000	2,000
Cudahy	5,500	3,300
FGE**	14,400	12,500
General American	8,100	5,300
Illinois Central	2,100	620
MDT	13,000	8,700
Morrell	640	800
National Car Co.***	1,700	1,200
North American	2,000	2,000
NRC	4,600	3,500
NWX	3,500	2,700
Northern Pacific	2,500	1,100
PFE	37,700	39,000
SFRD	14,100	14,800
SLRX	740	1,500
Swift	4,700	3,700
URTX*	7,500	4,100
Western	500	400
WFE**	7,100	5,700
Wilson	2,400	1,500

Key	
ART	American Refrigerator Transit (Missouri Pacific, Wabash)
BREX	Burlington Refrigerator Express (Burlington Route)
FGE	Fruit Growers Express (Atlantic Coast Line; Baltimore & Ohio; Central of Georgia; Chesapeake & Ohio; Chicago & Eastern Illinois; Florida East Coast; Louisville & Nashville; Nashville, Chattanooga & St. Louis; New Haven; Norfolk & Western; Norfolk Southern; Pennsylvania; Pere Marquette; Richmond, Fredericksburg & Potomac; Seaboard Air Line; Southern; and others)
MDT	Merchants Despatch Transit (Lackawanna, New York Central, Reading)
NRC	Northern Refrigerator Line (Illinois Central; Gulf, Mobile & Ohio; and others)
NWX	North Western Refrigerator Line (Chicago & North Western)
PFE	Pacific Fruit Express (Southern Pacific, Union Pacific, Western Pacific)
SFRD	Santa Fe Refrigerator Department (Atchison, Topeka & Santa Fe)
SLRX	St. Louis Refrigerator Car Co.
URTX	Union Refrigerator Transit (Milwaukee Road, Minneapolis & St. Louis, Rock Island, other railroads, and private owners)
Western	Western Refrigerator Line (Green Bay & Western)
WFE	Western Fruit Express

* URTX leased both produce and meat reefers to railroads and private owners. These numbers fluctuated; total URTX ownership is listed in both categories.

** BREX, FGE, and WFE operated as a cooperative and pooled cars.

*** National Car Co. was a subsidiary of FGE/BREX/WFE.

Many packing companies leased cars from General American, National Car Co., Union Refrigerator Transit, and others, and had these cars painted in the packing company scheme. These cars are listed with the leasing company.

USRA-style reefers, like this American Refrigerator Transit car, had deep fishbelly center sills (easily visible from the side), with wood-sheathed sides and ends. It's running in ventilator service, with its hatches propped open. *E. C. Heney, collection of J. Michael Gruber/Mainline Photos*

General American built many wood refrigerator cars from the 1920s through the 1940s. Leased to Minneapolis & St. Louis, this URTX car was built in 1931 and then rebuilt with steel ends in the early 1950s. *J. David Ingles collection*

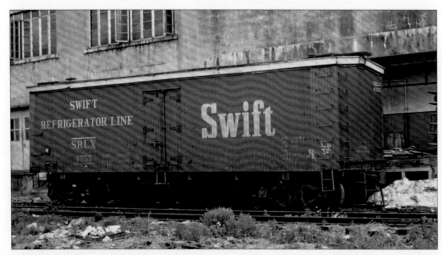

Swift operated a large fleet of 37-foot meat reefers with wood ends, sides, and roofs into the 1950s. The ends of the bolsters and crossbearers are visible under the sides. *Lloyd Keyser collection*

outside, but the cars were typically stenciled BRINE TANKS, and their AAR class, RA (or RAM with meat rails), also identified them.

Most meat reefers didn't serve as ventilator cars (and couldn't, in the case of brine tank cars), so the latch bars on the hatches didn't have notches like those on ventilator cars, and meat cars wouldn't be found rolling along with hatches propped open.

Another difference is that meat reefers rarely had air-circulating fans. Air circulated well in cars of hanging meat (compared with boxes of produce), while fans could dry hanging meat too quickly.

Meat and produce cars were operated in very different manners. Meat cars were owned or leased by specific packing companies, and served only that company. For example, a car owned or leased by Armour would never show up at a Swift or Wilson packing plant. It would travel exclusively from an Armour packing plant to a customer (such as an Armour branch house or food wholesaler), and then travel back to an Armour plant to be cleaned and reloaded.

Produce cars, on the other hand, could be found at a variety of packing houses and customers. A Fruit Growers Express car might receive a load of apples in Washington on one trip, and on the next trip, pick up a load of potatoes in Idaho or oranges in Florida.

Wood cars

By 1940, most boxcar (and other freight car) construction had shifted to all-steel designs. With refrigerator cars, the move to steel wasn't as quick. Many wood-sheathed cars continued to be built—albeit with steel ends and roofs—through the 1940s. Fruit Growers Express and Western Fruit Express both received orders of wood cars in 1946, and Swift received 200 wood-side (steel roof/end) cars in 1948.

Because there was no ARA or AAR standards, wood cars were built to many designs by several builders. Spotting features to look for are car length (many meat reefers were 36-footers) and height, door height, type of ends and roofs (similar to boxcars), style of roof hatches, running boards, style and size of side sills, underframe, and the style of grab irons and ladders (and number of rungs).

Since Pacific Fruit Express operated the largest fleet of cars, and its cars could be found on railroads across the country, its designs are probably the best known. Many of PFE's R-30-12 cars, which numbered almost 12,000 when built in the early 1920s, ran into the 1940s. More than 7,500 were still in service in 1940, and PFE had almost 6,000 similar R-30-13 cars running in 1940. (PFE car classes followed UP practice: the R was for refrigerator, the middle number was nominal capacity in tons, and the last number was the sequence of design for that capacity.)

Both classes had steel underframes and wood sides and ends, and all but the first R-30-12s had steel roofs. The underframes were not as deep as the USRA fishbelly underframe. The ends of the crossbearers were visible, as were the side sills below the wood sides.

Another common steel-underframe wood car found through the 1940s and '50s was the American Car & Foundry (ACF) design built for American Refrigerator Transit, UTLX, Western Refrigerator Lines, and others. These cars featured a fishbelly underframe, straight side sill, and wood ends.

General American was another prolific builder of wood refrigerator cars through the 1920s and '30s. These cars didn't have the deep underframes of the ACF cars.

Swift had a large fleet of 37-foot wood refrigerator cars, many of which operated through the 1950s (3,700 in 1948 and 2,100 in 1956). These cars had wood ends and roofs, and most had exposed I beam crossbearers visible below each side.

Although they represent older designs, Mather (which built and leased reefers, boxcars, and stock cars) operated a large fleet of reefers, with more than 1,300 still in service in the mid-1940s. Most of these 37-foot wood cars were leased to packing companies. Early cars had wood ends, while later ones had steel. They can be spotted by their exposed C-channel side sills.

Some wood meat reefers were built relatively late, such as this 37-foot Wilson car in 1948. Note the wood ends and exposed crossbearers. *J. David Ingles collection*

The 2,000 cars of the Pacific Fruit Express R-40-20 class were very similar on the outside to the R-40-10, with W corner post ends being the most apparent change. *Trains magazine collection*

The R-40-23 became PFE's largest class of steel reefers, with 5,000 cars. They had improved 3/3 Dreadnaught ends, air-circulating fans (note disk at lower left), and steel running boards. *E. C. Heney, collection of J. Michael Gruber/Mainline Photos*

AAR car codes for reefers		
Class R (Refrigerator cars)		
RS	Ice-bunker car	
RSM	Ice-bunker car with meat rails	
RA	Brine-tank car (usually for meat service)	
RAM	Brine-tank car with meat rails	
RB	Bunkerless car	
RC	Car carrying insulated containers	
RCD	Carbon-dioxide-cooled car	
RP	Mechanical refrigerator car	
RPA	Mechanical car powered by mechanical car-axle drive	
RPB	Mechanical car powered by electromechanical axle drive	
RT	Milk bulk car	

On the R-40-26 cars of 1950 and 1951, 6-foot-wide plug doors replaced swinging doors, which made it possible to use lift trucks. *J. David Ingles collection*

The Santa Fe car at right is a class Rr-28 reefer, one of 500 rebuilt from older USRA-design wood cars in 1940. It retains the deep fishbelly center sill from the original car (visible as a shadow). At left is a class Rr-53 car, one of 800 rebuilt in 1953 with plug doors. It's 7" taller than the older Rr-28. *Santa Fe*

Most wood sides comprised vertical boards, although some plywood-sheathed cars were built during World War II and after.

A significant number of wood reefers (even earlier wood-end and truss-underframe cars) lasted in service through the 1950s. For example, in 1940, about 34,000 of PFE's 38,000 cars were wood; by 1959, PFE still had about 12,000 wood cars (of about 32,000) in service.

Many wood cars were eventually rebuilt. Others were modernized over the years with updated components, including new trucks, AB brakes, steel running boards, and power brakes replacing vertical brake staffs.

Steel cars

Steel-sheathed cars were likewise built to many designs. Most followed the basic designs of contemporary ARA and AAR boxcars but with differences in individual components and details.

As with wood cars, PFE's steel designs are probably the best known, and PFE prototypes have been the focus of models in many scales. The first all-steel refrigerator cars were PFE's class R-40-10 cars built in 1936 and 1937. The first 700 of the 4,700 cars of this class were homebuilt; the rest were spread among five other builders. The R-40-10s were the second-largest group of ice cars owned by PFE.

The R-40-10s had square-post 4/4 Dreadnaught ends, riveted vertical steel side panels with tabs extending below the sides to cover the side bearer and bolster ends, steel panel roofs with wood running boards, and 4-foot-wide door openings with twin swinging doors. As these cars were reconditioned in the early 1950s, fans and steel running boards were added.

The next major series of PFE cars was the R-40-23 series. Built in 1947, the R-40-23s were the largest group of steel ice-bunker cars owned by PFE at 5,000 cars. As with the R-40-10s, PFE again turned to various builders (ACF, Pacific Car & Foundry, Pullman-Standard, General American, and Mount Vernon) for the cars.

These cars had improved 3/3 Dreadnaught ends with rounded corners (W corner posts), air-circulating fans, and convertible bunker walls. The steel sides had tabbed sills, and the cars had panel roofs with steel running boards. They stood about 3" taller than earlier cars and rode on ASF A-3 Ride Control trucks.

Another 3,000 cars were delivered in 1949 and 1950. These were class R-40-25, and were visually almost identical to the R-40-23 cars except for the addition of a diagonal-panel roof.

PFE's next car order was notable for ushering in the sliding plug door. Built in 1950–1951 (2,000 cars), the R-40-26 had 6-foot openings to allow lift trucks and loaders. Along with PFE, the reefers of many other owners would receive plug doors through the 1950s.

The Santa Fe (SFRD) would also acquire a large fleet of steel refrigerator cars, but most would be cars rebuilt from older wood cars (more on that in a bit). The first batch of new SFRD cars, class Rr-21 (500 cars), was built in 1937; another 1,100 new steel cars were built through 1953.

Another common steel car was the horizontal side seam design, which first appeared in 1939. Instead of vertical steel panels comprising the sides, these cars had horizontal side panels with the top panel overlapping the bottom panel, which created a distinctive horizontal rivet seam.

American Refrigerator Transit initially built 775 of these cars (from ACF kits), which had square-corner 4/4 Dreadnaught ends. In 1947 and 1948, ART built or ordered (from Pullman-Standard and General American) another 2,296 cars, this time with improved 3/4 ends.

General American and Pacific Car & Foundry built a number of similar cars for Armour and URTX (which leased them to railroads and packing companies) from the late 1940s into the 1950s. A variation was a 770-car batch of 39-footers with double-latch bars built in 1954 for Swift.

Many other railroads and private owners had significant fleets of steel cars. Spotting features include door size and style, side sill (straight or tabbed), ends, roof, hatch design, ladders and grab irons, and length.

By the mid-1950s, the use of mechanical reefers increased for carrying conventional perishable traffic as well as for frozen food. Tractor-trailers were making a dent in perishable traffic as well, thanks to increased trailer size and the growth of the Interstate Highway system. Few new ice-bunker cars were built after

American Refrigerator Transit operated more than 3,000 40-foot steel cars with horizontal side seams. The cars had tabs over the crossbearer and bolster ends. *J. David Ingles collection*

General American built many 42-foot steel refrigerator cars with horizontal side seams and tabbed sills in the 1940s and 1950s. This URTX car is leased to Milwaukee Road. *Dean Hale, collection of Jay Williams/Big Four Graphics*

In 1954, General American built more than 700 39-foot steel cars for Swift. The sides had horizontal side seams, and the doors featured a unique double-latch bar design. *J. David Ingles collection*

This Illinois Central "banana reefer" was one of 500 steel cars delivered in 1937 and 1940. Built by General American, it has tabbed sills, Dreadnaught ends, an arched eave over the door, and cooling fans (a 1950s addition). *J. David Ingles collection*

The first 250 plug-door ice cars for Burlington Refrigerator Express were built in 1951. These steel cars had straight side sills, improved Dreadnaught ends, and diagonal-panel roofs. *Collection of Jay Williams/Big Four Graphics*

Built in 1947, this Merchants Despatch car is one of a batch of 1,000 steel ice-bunker cars built with extra-heavy insulation designed for hauling frozen foods. The 40-foot car has tabbed sills. *New York Central*

the mid-1950s; PFE received its last ice car in 1957.

50-foot cars

Most ice-bunker refrigerator cars were 36 to 42 feet long, but some 50-foot cars were built prior to the coming of mechanical reefers and insulated boxcars. Shippers tended to favor the shorter cars, but some general-purpose 50-footers were built.

However, one type of 50-foot car, known as a super-insulated reefer, was built specifically to carry frozen food, a rapidly expanding segment of the ready-made food market. Frozen food must be maintained below zero to remain solid and retain freshness, a temperature that pushed the limits of ice-bunker cars. Below-zero temperatures were possible, however, by combining ice with a lot of salt added to the bunker. To better maintain the low temperature, many 50-foot cars were built with extra-thick insulation.

The Santa Fe had built 100 standard 50-footers (class Rr-10) in 1931, and rebuilt 10 of these with heavy insulation in 1936. The Santa Fe ordered 200 steel, heavy-insulation 50-foot cars from General American in 1937, followed by another 150 in 1940 and 75 rebuilt Rr10 cars.

The first 50-footers for PFE were the wood-sheathed R-70-2 cars, a 100-car series built in 1932. PFE followed with another 1,000 or so wood-sheathed 50-foot cars, plus another 187 steel 50-footers in the early 1950s.

Other operators also had small numbers of 50-foot cars, including FGE, which had some overhead-bunker cars (more on those later).

Rebuilt cars

As with boxcars, older wood refrigerator cars were rebuilt, many with steel components. The Santa Fe Refrigerator Department in particular rebuilt most of its older wood cars with steel bodies. The SFRD rebuilt more than 10,000 cars from 1936 to 1950, mostly early USRA-design cars that were initially built in the early 1920s. These can be spotted by their fishbelly underframes that were retained after rebuilding.

Because they were rebuilt over such a long period, many differences in details exist among groups of the cars. These include early Dreadnaught ends that became improved Dreadnaughts on later cars. Panel roofs were used on early cars and changed to diagonal-panel roofs later. A narrow flat area along the top of each side became wider during production. Running boards were wood on early rebuilds, with a hatch platform that went from surrounding the hatch on early cars to just being on the inside area. Metal running boards then appeared on later cars. Trucks varied as some rebuilds retained Andrews trucks, while others got ASF A-3 trucks.

The Santa Fe also rebuilt about 2,800 older ARA-style (straight center sill, ARA-style underframe) cars from 1950 to 1954. These cars were about 8" taller than earlier rebuilds, and they received sliding plug doors instead of swinging doors.

PFE also rebuilt and reconditioned several thousand cars from the late 1930s through the 1940s. Unlike the Santa Fe, PFE rebuilds kept their wood side sheathing (including a batch with plywood sheathing, the R-30-24 and R-40-24 classes in 1947). Rebuilds received new steel (Dreadnaught) ends and roofs with upgraded hardware.

Older wood cars from ART, FGE, MDT, and others were also rebuilt during this period. Basic upgrades included AB brakes that replaced earlier K brakes and new trucks to replace older Andrews and T-section Bettendorf trucks. As with the Santa Fe and PFE cars, extensive rebuilding included new ends, sides, and roofs.

Mechanical refrigerator cars

The introduction of mechanical refrigerator cars was spurred not by fruit, vegetable, or meat traffic, but by the growing frozen food industry. Frozen food production in the United States jumped from about 514,000 tons in 1945 to 2 million tons in 1954. The biggest share of this was in frozen concentrated juice, which grew from 226,000 gallons in 1945 to 70 million gallons in 1954.

This 50-foot car is one of 50 Rr-31 super-insulated cars built in 1940 for frozen-food service. Precooling motors are attached to the fan housings at each end. *Santa Fe*

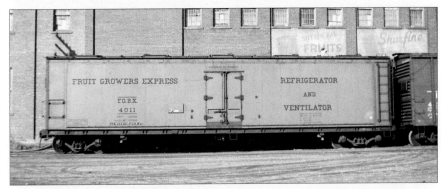

This 50-foot car was one of about 200 overhead-bunker cars operated by Fruit Growers Express. The steel car had 10 roof hatches, a straight visible side sill, and a deep fishbelly underframe. *G. W. Sisk, collection of Jay Williams/Big Four Graphics*

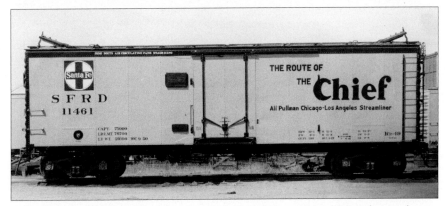

Santa Fe's class Rr-49 steel reefers were rebuilt with from older ARA-style wood cars in 1950. This car has a sliding plug door, improved Dreadnaught 3/4 ends, and a panel roof. *Santa Fe*

Ice-bunker cars—even the super-insulated 50-footers—simply couldn't do a good enough job of holding frozen lading to the below-zero temperatures required. Seeing the growth in the frozen food industry and the potential for traffic, refrigerator-car operators began experimenting with mechanical refrigeration.

Fruit Growers Express handled much of the Florida citrus market and

saw good potential for concentrate traffic. In 1948, FGE, with its partners BRE and WFE, tested several refrigeration systems, including ammonia, dry ice, and diesel- and gas-powered refrigeration units, in 16 cars. The diesel-powered units proved to be the best option, and became standard for mechanical refrigerators.

Mechanical cars use a small diesel engine to turn an alternator, which

The 2,400 cars of PFE class R-40-24 (shown) and R-30-24 received plywood sheathing when rebuilt in 1948. You can see the seams between panels. These cars had exposed ends on crossbearers and bolsters. *Collection of Jay Williams/Big Four Graphics*

Western Fruit Express no. 8073 was one of 150 mechanical reefers built for WFE in 1955. The vents on the right side show the location of the refrigeration equipment. The 52-foot car has a 6-foot plug door, straight side sills, and roller-bearing trucks. *J. David Ingles collection*

Canadian railroads began operating large numbers of overhead-bunker cars in the 1940s. This 42-foot car is one of a series of 190 built with plug doors in 1958. *Canadian National*

powers the refrigeration equipment (compressor, condenser, evaporator) and circulation fans. The units can provide heat as well, regulating the temperature automatically regardless of outside temperature. The refrigeration equipment resides in an end of the car, marked by vented louvers or grates low on the car side.

This technology came at a steep initial price: in 1953, PFE's first mechanical reefers cost $21,200 each, compared to $13,400 for an ice car.

By 1955, about 1,200 mechanical cars were in service. The FGE/BRE/WFE group had almost 600 mechanical cars. PFE, which started with 25 in 1953, had about 330 by 1955. SFRD started with 30 in 1953 and had 180 by 1955. Refrigeration equipment came from Thermo-King, Trane, Frigidaire, Waukesha, and Carrier.

Mechanical reefers proved to be reliable and efficient. Interior temperature was automatically controlled, and the engine/refrigeration units could operate two weeks or more before needing refueling.

The efficiency of the refrigeration equipment, together with improving materials and techniques in insulation and construction, led to larger cars. Although some 40-foot mechanical reefers were built, 50 feet became common. With this size increase came a capacity increase, from the 30 or 40 tons of a typical ice car to 50 or 70 tons.

Designs paralleled those of contemporary boxcars and insulated boxcars, with Dreadnaught ends and diagonal-panel roofs. Straight side sills were common, with some having tabbed side sills as on AAR boxcars. Plug doors of various types were standard on mechanical cars. Six-foot-wide openings were initially the most common, but 8-foot doors became popular from the late 1950s into the 1960s. Cushioned draft gear and underframes were used to protect the cased lading.

Most mechanical cars through the 1950s had smooth steel sides, made of riveted vertical sheets, just like contemporary boxcars. It wasn't until the 1960s that larger reefers with exterior side posts became common.

The eight roof hatches are shown evenly spaced on the overhead-bunker ice cars. *Canadian National*

Several experimental aluminum refrigerator cars were built in the 1940s, including Fruit Growers Express no. 40000 in 1946. Cars generally followed contemporary construction but with aluminum substituted for steel. *Fruit Growers Express*

Additional spotting features include the location of vents (and louvers or screened openings) and rooftop exhaust pipes and the style and location of underslung fuel tanks. Mechanical reefers were among the early users of roller-bearing trucks—many received them when built in the 1950s.

By the end of the 1950s, most mechanical cars were used for frozen goods, but a growing number were used in fruit and vegetable traffic. Even with the success of mechanical cars, they remained a small portion of reefers in the transition era. Of a total of about 120,000 cars, about 5,000 were in service by 1960. Looking at the largest fleet, of PFE's 29,000 reefers, only about 2,000 were mechanical.

Canadian and other overhead-bunker cars

Unlike U.S. railroads, Canadian railroads owned the refrigerator cars operating on their lines. One innovation adopted widely by Canadian lines was the overhead ice bunker, with tanks mounted in the ceiling instead of in the ends. The Canadian Pacific began this practice with 50 wood-sheathed cars in 1938. Construction soon switched to steel, and by 1950, about 3,000 overhead-bunker cars were in service.

These cars used wide, shallow brine tanks instead of bunkers, as drainage would have been problematic with conventional bunkers above loads in

cars. Externally, the steel-side cars had tabs over crossbearers, 4-foot wide doors (which were shorter than other cars to allow for the overhead brine tanks), and eight roof hatches allowing access to eight brine tanks. The design was updated over the years, and changes included a move from swinging doors to a sliding plug door around 1950.

These cars were all equipped with meat rails, as meat was a more common shipment than produce or vegetables on Canadian lines. The design proved efficient for this service in both cooling and use of floor space. The tanks had a 7,000-pound capacity, compared to 9,000–11,000 pounds for a comparable end-bunker car. Flues in the walls and below the tanks aided airflow.

The cars were also equipped with permanent underbody heaters. To heat a standard bunker car, a portable heater was lowered into the end bunkers.

Some U.S. refrigerator-car operators, including PFE, FGE, and ART, experimented with overhead-bunker cars, but the design didn't prove popular. Downsides included possible load contamination from leaking tanks or drain pans and the more time-consuming icing process the cars presented at docks. Brine tanks also didn't allow for ventilator service or

fans, and more airflow was required for produce lading.

Experimental aluminum cars

As with boxcars, builders experimented with aluminum as a building material in the 1940s, to limited response. New aluminum ice-bunker cars included Fruit Growers Express 40000, built in 1946 (equipped with Timken roller-bearing trucks), and Illinois Central 51000, also built in 1946, with Alcoa aluminum and equipped with a Duryea cushion underframe.

Pacific Fruit Express rebuilt two earlier steel-side cars (class R-40-14) with aluminum bodies in 1946 and 1947. The first, no. 45698, had material from Reynolds; the second, no. 44739, had aluminum from Alcoa.

In 1958, Canadian National no. 212200, a 40-foot, 60-ton car with plug doors and overhead bunkers, was built by Aluminum Limited.

Another one-of-a-kind car is SFRD no. 13000, a stainless-steel car built in 1946 by Consolidated Steel Corp., with the idea that stainless steel would better resist corrosion from ice and salt.

Although these cars performed well, and most had long service lives, railroads determined the initial high cost of the components wasn't sufficiently offset by savings in weight or maintenance.

CHAPTER FIVE

Hoppers and gondolas

Two iconic coal haulers of the transition era—twin-bay offset-side and exterior-post hopper cars—take on loads at a mine tipple along the Louisville & Nashville in 1954. *William A. Akin*

Hopper cars and gondolas were the second- and third-most common car types of the transition era. The hopper was synonymous with coal car, but it also carried aggregates and other materials. Gondolas also carried coal as well as steel components, scrap, and pretty much anything else that wouldn't easily fit inside an enclosed car.

Hopper cars

From the steam era through the 1940s and 1950s, the hopper car was the standard coal car, carrying black diamonds from mines to power plants, steel mills and other industries, export docks, and local coal dealers.

Solid trains of hoppers could be found along railroads, including the Norfolk & Western, Virginian, and Chesapeake & Ohio, that operated among Appalachian and other coalfields. This was a period before unit trains, so cars in these trains were waybilled individually and could be headed to a variety of destinations.

A hopper car is basically an open box on wheels, with ends and floors that slope downward to outlet doors or gates in two or more bays, or hoppers. Because of the strength required for the abuse they take in loading, hopper cars were among the first all-steel cars, with steel sides and ends, bracing, and frame (center sill).

Hopper cars are typically described by their number of bays and their nominal capacity. (Two-bay cars are also called twin hoppers, three-bay cars are triple hoppers, and four-bay cars are quad hoppers.)

USRA hoppers

The forerunners to contemporary transition-era hoppers were United States Railroad Administration (USRA) hoppers, which proved to be among the most common hopper cars in service from the 1920s into the 1940s. During USRA control of U.S. railroads during and immediately after World War I, the USRA developed designs for a two-bay, 55-ton car and a three-bay, 70-ton car.

The two-bay, 55-ton hopper in particular proved extremely popular. The all-steel car was an exterior-post (outside-braced) design, with seven vertical posts on each side. The car measured 30 feet long and 10'-8" tall and had a volume capacity of 1,880 cubic feet (cf).

More than 22,000 of these cars were built under USRA direction, and another 28,000 clones (identical or very similar cars) were built to the design, mainly during the 1920s. A majority were still in

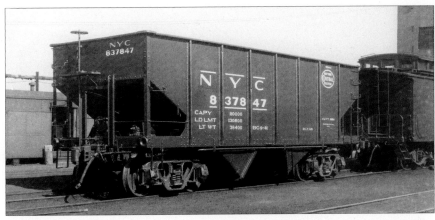

The USRA twin hopper was one of the most common coal carriers through the 1930s, and many lasted through the 1950s. *Trains magazine collection*

Many USRA hoppers were rebuilt with projecting panels between the side posts. This Wabash car was built in 1923 and rebuilt in 1936. *Trains magazine collection*

Three-bay, 70-ton USRA hoppers had twin middle discharge gates set higher than the outside hoppers. This Chesapeake & Ohio car was built in 1923. *Chesapeake & Ohio*

service in 1940, and many lasted through the 1950s and into the 1960s.

Many of these cars were upgraded and rebuilt beginning in the 1930s, with the addition of AB brakes (to replace the original K brakes), geared hand brakes (replacing vertical-staff brake wheels), new trucks, and the replacement of hardware as needed, such as new outlet gates or side panels.

Several thousand of these cars received panel sides during rebuilding. These protruding side panels fit between the exterior posts and gave cars

45

This Monon car, built in 1954, is an AAR standard offset-side car, with angle stiffeners spaced unevenly and a 2,145-cubic-foot capacity. *Trains magazine collection*

Three-bay offset-side hoppers had a 70-ton capacity. This Burlington car, built in 1953, has a 2,773-cf capacity. *J. David Ingles collection*

This Minneapolis & St. Louis car is built to the AAR alternate standard, with a 10'-5" height and evenly spaced stiffeners. This car shows the stamped (hat-shaped) stiffeners. It was built in 1936. *Minneapolis & St. Louis*

a distinctive appearance. The panels increased side strength and upped the cubic capacity to 1,954 cubic feet.

The three-bay USRA cars weren't as popular, as not all routes in the 1920s could handle 70-ton cars. None were built at USRA direction, but five railroads bought 21,000 cars of the design in the 1920s. The cars were still 10'-8" tall but were stretched to 40'-5" long, giving them a 2,508-cf capacity.

These cars had nine vertical posts on each side and were distinctive in that the center bay had twin discharge doors set higher than the end "saw-tooth" bays, which had doors only on the side facing the center of the car. As with the two-bay cars, most of these cars were later upgraded and rebuilt.

Offset-side cars

As with boxcars, beginning in the 1920s, the American Railway Association (the American Association of Railroads from 1934 onward) developed standard designs for hopper cars. These were updated and refined over the years, and could be used by any manufacturer.

The ARA settled on an offset-side design for their initial designs, with the vertical side posts on the interior and steel sheathing on the outside. The side angled back in toward the interior at the top, with triangular stiffeners along the outside top edge at the angle. This design increased a car's cubic capacity compared to an otherwise-identical outside-braced car.

The bottom of each bay angled down to a pair of outlet gates (one gate or door on each side of the center sill). This means a two-bay car had four doors and a three-bay car had six.

Both 50- and 70-ton versions were developed. The first design, proposed in 1926 and then revised slightly and approved in 1929, was for a 70-ton, four-bay, 40-foot-long car. Although not nearly as popular as the later 50-ton versions, almost 14,000 of these cars were built through 1930, and a majority remained in service (albeit rebuilt and reconditioned) into the 1960s.

The first 50-ton ARA offset-side version adopted was for a 35-foot-long, three-bay car. This three-bay design was unusual for such a short car, and very few were built. The later two-bay design proved far more popular.

The next revision to these designs, by the AAR in 1934, marked the start of what would be the most popular hopper cars through the transition era. The 50-ton car was revised with two bays, and most had a volume capacity of 2,145 cubic feet—almost 200 cubic feet more than a USRA car. Each side had nine angle stiffeners along the top, spaced unevenly (due to the locations of the interior vertical posts, which varied based on where the slope sheets met the bottom of the sides).

The 70-ton car was likewise modified with one fewer bay, becoming a 41-foot, three-bay car with a 2,773-cf capacity. This car had 10 stiffeners, or gussets, across the top of each side.

Both of these designs proved extremely popular, with 50-ton cars being built starting in 1934 and 70-tonners in 1938. By the mid-1950s, about 127,000 of the 50-ton cars and 32,000 70-ton cars had been built.

Variations

Throughout production, many details were changed and updated, and other details varied by railroad and builder. A significant change was the next major revision to the AAR design in 1946, when the car length and truck spacing were both increased—by 2 feet on the 50-ton car and 1 foot on the 70-ton car.

An easy-to-see variation involved the angled stiffeners that ran along the tops of the sides. Early cars had stamped-metal (sometimes called *hat-shaped*) pieces, as on the Minneapolis & St. Louis 50-ton car shown on the opposite page, and some later cars also had these. Most cars built after 1934 had metal angles, as on the Monon car on page 46.

The spacing of these angles also varied. Many 50-ton cars were built to an alternate standard that was shorter in height (10'-5" instead of 10'-8"), and these cars had angles that were more evenly spaced.

Hopper doors and door locks varied, with the two most common being manufactured by Enterprise or Wine. Enterprise latches had individual latches for each door, while Wine locks had bars across both paired doors that allowed them to be opened together. Some cars had side sills that were straight pieces from the truck bolster to the end; on other cars, this piece angled upward.

As with other hopper cars, some offset-side cars were built with heap shields. These angled or curved extensions to the ends protected a higher load of coal from falling out of the ends. Starting in 1942, these shields were notched above the end ladders.

Some offset-side cars were not built to AAR standards. The main spotting features on these cars include having

This view shows the interior vertical posts of offset-side cars, along with the angle bracing. *New York Central*

This Louisville & Nashville 2,092-cf car is a non-AAR standard car, with seven stiffeners and end panels with abrupt angles instead of gradual ones. *Louisville & Nashville*

Bethlehem built this 55-ton, two-bay car for Lehigh Valley in 1939. Several eastern roads had cars with fishbelly style sides like this 1,860-cf car. *Bethlehem*

just seven angled pieces along the sides, and the end panel on each side having an abrupt angle where it meets the side angle (as opposed to the gradual taper on AAR cars). The L&N car shown above also has side sills at the end that are much thicker than a standard car.

Offset-side cars were vulnerable to damage, as loading could knock the sides away from the interior posts and cause them to buckle outward. As they sustained various levels of damage over the years, these cars were often rebuilt with new sides.

ACF built this welded two-bay car for Lackawanna in 1949. The 50-ton exterior-post car has a 2,221-cf capacity. *ACF*

Construction of these cars tapered off in the mid-1950s, as railroads moved toward 70-ton and larger cars and shifted toward outside-braced designs.

Exterior-post cars

Although the offset-side car was extremely popular, tens of thousands of 50- and 70-ton exterior-post cars were also built to several designs. Although outside-braced cars didn't have as much capacity as offset-side cars, they were sturdier and less prone to side damage since the sheathing was inside the posts.

Many railroads had large fleets of cars utilizing both designs, while some railroads—such as the Pennsylvania and Norfolk & Western—preferred their own designs for exterior-post cars. Some railroads also operated heavier cars, but kept them strictly on their own lines, as the Virginian and the N&W did, since the 1910s, with their 100-ton cars.

As with offset-side cars, exterior-post hoppers in the transition era were predominantly two-bay (50- or 55-ton) or three-bay (70-ton) cars. Key

spotting features are their height and length, number of side posts, along with the posts' shape and depth, and the angle of slope on the end sheets. Other details are much like other hopper cars: trucks, ends (heap shields or straight), brakes, door hardware, and end bracing.

As railroads began shifting toward outside-braced cars in the mid-1950s, the AAR followed. In 1957, several eastern railroads developed a 70-ton triple hopper with exterior posts and an inside length of 40'-8", which became an AAR standard design in 1960.

Into the 1950s, most hoppers were riveted, but welded exterior-post cars began appearing in the late 1940s. Both American Car & Foundry (ACF) and Pullman-Standard offered versions of 50-ton, two-bay cars with welded superstructures.

Pullman-Standard in 1953 introduced its PS-3 hopper car. As with PS-1 boxcars and PS-2 covered hoppers, PS-3 covers all of the company's hoppers, regardless of size.

AAR car codes for hoppers	
Class H (Hopper car types)	
HM	Twin-bottom car
HMA	Twin-bottom car with lengthwise (between-rails) doors
HE	Non-self-clearing car
HT	Three-bottom (or more) car
HTA	Three-bottom (or more) car with lengthwise (between rails) doors
HD	Two-bottom (or more) car with lengthwise (outside rails) doors
HK	Two-bottom (or more) car with lengthwise (between rails or outside rails) doors

War-emergency cars

World War II created a major shortage of steel for products not directly related to the war effort. Railroads and builders in need of new cars often had to turn to alternate materials. The AAR approved an emergency design for a 50-ton, two-bay composite hopper with external truss-style bracing and wood sheathing (horizontal planks). About 10,000 were built in the early 1940s.

The design called for the wood sheathing to eventually be replaced with steel sheets. This was done on many cars through the 1950s, but some cars continued in service with wood sides into the 1960s.

Ore cars

Ore cars are hopper cars designed specifically for carrying iron ore or processed taconite pellets. Because ore is extremely dense—more than 160 pounds per cubic foot, compared to around 55 pounds per cubic foot of coal—loading a standard hopper car with ore would grossly overload it.

Ore cars were thus designed with much smaller cubic capacity, even though their weight limits in the 1940s and 1950s were usually 50 or 70 tons, as with a standard hopper car.

Most ore cars were in service in the ore ranges of the upper Midwest, mainly northern Minnesota and Michigan's upper peninsula, and on lines from the southern Great Lakes to the steel centers of Ohio and Pennsylvania. The cars were used to haul ore from mines and processing plants to ships, and then from shipping docks to mills.

Ore cars travel in packs, usually in dedicated trains, and you would rarely see single cars mixed in with general freight.

These cars followed several designs that varied by railroad. Top ore car owners included Duluth, Missabe & Iron Range, Great Northern, Chicago & North Western, Soo Line, Lake Superior & Ishpeming, and Pennsylvania Railroad.

Cars were generally 21 feet long (to match the unloading pockets in lake shipping docks), with capacities around 900–1,000 cubic feet. Most had bodies that tapered to a single lengthwise

The Norfolk & Western built more than 13,000 outside-braced class H2A hoppers like this one at its Roanoke shops. The 70-ton, three-bay car has a 2,460-cf capacity. *John B. Corns collection*

The PS-3 was Pullman's standard welded line of hopper cars. The two-bay, 50-ton version had a 2,134-cf capacity. *Pullman-Standard*

Rock Island no. 9073 is a three-bay, 70-ton Pullman-Standard PS-3 hopper built in 1957. The welded car has a 2,750-cf capacity. *Pullman-Standard*

War-emergency hoppers had steel-truss side bracing with interior wood plank sheathing. Bethlehem built this two-bay version for the Baltimore & Ohio in 1943. *Baltimore & Ohio*

Aluminum companies made a push at freight cars in the 1940s. Chesapeake & Ohio no. 130 is one of five such offset-side, two-bay cars built in the company's Russell, Ky., shops in 1948. Note the notched oval heap shield. *Chesapeake & Ohio*

and other bulky goods that won't fit into a boxcar. In fact, a good share of the fun in modeling gondolas is modeling the loads that go into them.

During the transition era, gondolas were the third-most common car type behind boxcars and hoppers. Although most AAR reports combine hoppers and gons in roster totals into the 1950s, about 338,000 gondolas were running in 1943 and 293,000 in 1955.

Through the transition era, gondolas fell into two basic categories—mill and general service—and each had a variety of subclasses that made them suitable for carrying different goods.

As with hopper cars, steel became the primary building material for gondolas, although plenty of composite-side cars were built. About 20,000 composite (wood-side, steel-frame) cars were built to USRA designs during World War I and the years after, and some of these lasted into the transition era. Some composite gons were built during the 1930s and then during World War II because of steel shortages.

From the 1920s through the '30s, gons were built to a number of designs that varied by railroad and builder. It wasn't until early World War II (1941 and 1942) that the AAR adopted designs for several types of gondolas, including both steel and composite-side cars.

Mill gondolas

As the name implies, mill gondolas are designed primarily to carry products that serve steel mills—scrap metal going in, and finished beams, sheets, and other goods going out—but they can haul other loads as well.

Mill gons fall under AAR class GB, which is a gondola with a solid floor, solid sides, and fixed or drop ends. Mill gondolas are typically longer than general-service cars, at lengths from 40 to 65 feet, with a capacity of 50 or 70 tons. To save on car weight, the longer a mill gondola is, the lower its sides are.

By 1941 and 1942, the AAR had these recommended-practice designs for steel mill gons:

- 42-foot, 50-ton, fixed end
- 52-foot, 70-ton, drop end
- 65-foot, 70-ton, drop end

bottom opening. Spotting features include the sides (smooth with vertical posts or with offset sides) and the shape and style of the side and end bracing.

Ballast cars

Another type of specialized hopper car is the ballast car. These cars look much like a standard hopper, but their outlet doors run lengthwise, and they can be adjusted to dump their loads between the rails or outside them. They are AAR class HTA, HD, or HK, depending upon the style of

bottom doors. Along with being in maintenance-of-way service, they can be found in revenue service hauling rock, aggregate, and other products.

Gondolas

Gondolas are multipurpose cars that carry a tremendous variety of products. Some railroads preferred gondolas to hoppers for carrying bulk commodities such as coal, limestone, and other aggregates. Other gons carry scrap metal; new products such as steel beams, lumber, and pipe; or machinery

These cars followed basic designs that had been produced for several years. The 42-foot car was also a common coal carrier, especially for railroads that served lake shipping terminals and other customers with rotary dumpers.

The sides of mill gondolas act as girders in the car's strength. Vertical members (steel angles or stamped shapes) are riveted or welded along the exterior of each side. The sides on 40-foot (and tall-side 50-foot cars) usually have straight bottoms. On 50-foot and longer cars (hence, lower sides), they usually taper down lower between the trucks (called *fishbelly sides*) to provide extra strength.

Floors were typically either solid steel or wood planks. A few cars in this period had nailable steel floors—horizontal steel shapes with small gaps between them where nails could be driven. Railroads ordering cars primarily for coal service usually specified solid steel.

Floors are sometimes fitted with racks or other loading devices in cars designed to carry a specific load, such as coiled steel, auto frames, containers, or other dedicated products.

Some gons are equipped with folding stake pockets on the interior sides; others have tie-down clips along the outside edge of the bulb angle (the lip that runs atop the side). Another loading device was the Wine lading band, a corrugated series of anchors attached along the top of each side.

Mill gons can have drop ends—ends that could be released and collapsed inward to the car floor. This allows cars to carry loads that are longer than the car itself, such as pipes, beams, and other structural shapes. When this was done, an idler flatcar was placed next to the gon to clear the ends of the load.

On drop-end gons, a brake lever (or pump-style handle) usually takes the place of a brake wheel and is mounted on the end of the side so that it clears the end and the end opening. Some drop-end cars use standard brake wheels, mounted on the end of the side and parallel to the car (see the Santa Fe car on page 53).

Ore cars varied in design among railroads. Chicago & North Western no. 121641 is a 70-ton ore car built in 1926. These cars remained in service into the 1960s. *Trains magazine collection*

This 70-ton Milwaukee Road car was built in 1930. Note the slab sides, compared to the exterior posts on the C&NW car. *Pressed Steel Car Co.*

Ballast cars have longitudinal gates that can drop their load between the rails or outside them. This ACF Hart Selective ballast car was built in 1937. *ACF*

51

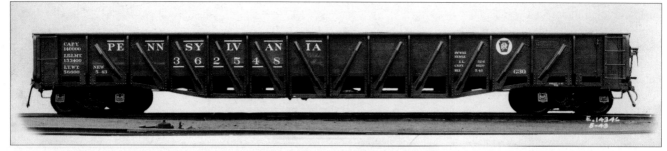

This war-emergency mill gondola is 53 feet long and has steel-truss framing with wood sheathing. It was built in 1943. *Pennsylvania Railroad*

This 42-foot New York Central gondola has a slight fishbelly shape at the bottom of the sides. It was built in the 1920s and rebuilt in 1952. *Chuck Yungkurth collection*

This 42-foot, 50-ton, fixed-end gondola is one of an order of 400 built by ACF for Seaboard Air Line in 1949. *ACF*

AAR car codes for gondolas	
Class G (Gondola car types)	
GB	Mill gondola, fixed or drop ends
GT	Coal gondola, high sides and fixed ends
GA	Drop-bottom (between rails) car, fixed ends
GE	Drop-bottom (between rails) car, drop ends
GH	Drop-bottom (outside of rails) car, drop ends
GS	Drop-bottom (outside of rails) car, fixed ends
GRA	Drop-hopper-bottom car, fixed ends and sides
GD	Side-dump car
GW	Well-hole car

Gondolas featured riveted construction into the 1940s, but by the late 1940s, cars with some welded components began to appear. Welded construction became more popular by the late 1950s.

Among the most common mill gons was a 52'-6" design first built by Greenville in 1940. By 1957, almost 16,000 had been built by several builders. The cars had 14 side posts and a 7'-4" height to the top of the sides (7'-1" on a few cars).

Spotting features for mill gons include length and height, the number of vertical posts, the style of posts (angled or stamped), length of posts, welded or riveted construction, rivet patterns, and grab irons or ladders at the corners.

Ends are another spotting feature. Gondola ends followed contemporary boxcar designs, albeit shorter. Dreadnaught ends in various styles were standard by 1940, with Murphy ends found on many earlier cars. Pullman-Standard developed its own straight-rib end, as it did with its boxcar design. Ends on cars in coal service sometimes had raised heap shields as on hopper cars.

Another type of fixed-end, solid-floor car was the AAR class GT, specified as a coal gondola. Although many cars in coal service were simply classified GB, most of the GT cars were built specifically for coal service, especially in the early 1900s on several eastern roads, including Norfolk & Western and Virginian. Many were designed strictly for on-line use with high capacities (up to 100 tons) and often with six-wheel trucks. These cars were the forerunners of today's 110-ton coal cars.

The brake wheel on this drop-bottom, 53-foot mill gondola is positioned off the end of the car for clearance. ACF built the 70-ton, riveted car in 1949 for the Santa Fe. *ACF*

General-service gons

General-service gondolas had drop bottoms—specifically, a number of doors along each side of the floor that opened to allow clearing a load. By far the most common type was the 41-foot GS car. Most had 16 doors (eight on each lengthwise half of the floor), although some had 12 doors. The doors were located on either side of the center sill, and between the bolsters and side bearers on the underframe. Each door hinged at the side nearest the car center, so the outside of the door dropped down, dumping the lading outside the rails.

Other versions had bottoms that dropped between the rails, and there were cars with drop ends as well.

General-service gons would carry any number of products, but they were quite popular for coal service, especially among western railroads. Many railroads preferred GS gondolas to hoppers for hauling coal, as these cars could be used for other products when not in coal service.

A popular early variation was the Caswell gondola, a composite-side, drop-bottom car operated in large numbers exclusively by the Santa Fe. The car had truss-style steel side framing with horizontal interior wood sheathing.

The railroad owned more than 8,000 of these cars, which were built through the late 1920s. Although owned by the ATSF, these distinctive cars traveled throughout the country. Many remained in service—albeit

ACF built this welded 53-foot, fixed-end mill gon for the Pennsy in 1952. Tie-down clips run along the outside edge of the bulb angle at the top of the side. *ACF*

Built in 1957 by Pullman-Standard, this Rock Island gondola has drop ends, a lever-style brake handle, and a Wine lading band anchoring system along the top of each side. *Pullman-Standard*

Drop-bottom gons allow loads much longer than the car itself. Idler flatcars provide spacing between these beam loads. *J. David Ingles collection*

Caswell gondolas were composite-side, drop-bottom cars exclusive to the Santa Fe. Here, a steam locomotive pulls a train of empties near Raton, N.M. *Santa Fe*

This Northern Pacific GS gondola was built in 1940. It has an interior height of 4'-5". The rods and chains at the base of the side control the drop doors. *Stan Mailer*

rebuilt and upgraded—through the transition era.

Steel general-service gons followed similar lines. They had an inside length of 41'-0" but could vary in height, ranging from an inside height of 4'-5" to 5'-6" or even taller for cars designed to carry wood chips, with common cubic capacities from 1,750 to 2,124 cubic feet.

Most GS gons had seven vertical exterior posts. Sides could be flat to the bottom or angled inward at the bottom. A door-operating bar ran lengthwise below each side, with chains and links that opened and closed the doors. The operating lever was on the end of the car at the end of each bar.

War-emergency cars

As with boxcars and hopper cars, the AAR issued war-emergency composite designs for gondolas that featured steel truss framing, wood interior side sheathing, and wood floors. These included a 41-foot (41'-6" inside length), 50-ton, fixed-end, solid-bottom car; a 52-foot, 70-ton, drop-end, solid-bottom car; and a 41-foot, fixed-end, drop-bottom car.

The most common version built, with 5,500 cars, was the 41-foot, solid-bottom car, followed by the 52-foot car with about 2,900. As with other war-emergency car types, railroads rebuilt many of these cars with steel sides and floors through the 1950s.

This home-shop-built Soo Line car has sides that angle in at the base. The 50-ton, drop-bottom car has an inside height of 4'-11". *Trains magazine collection*

CHAPTER SIX

Tank cars

Tank cars were among the first steel railcars, and their basic design remained largely unchanged from the 1910s into the 1950s. They could be found in most freight trains carrying petroleum products, various chemicals and industrial solvents, and food products such as corn syrup and vegetable oil.

This early ACF Type 17 tank car, built in 1917, was still going strong in the 1940s hauling petroleum products. Early cars had tanks made from a bottom longitudinal sheet, with several radial courses (five in this case), identified by the rivets at the seams. This is a 10,000-gallon, 50-ton car. *G. W. Sisk, collection of Jay Williams/Big Four Graphics*

Unlike later cars, ACF's Type 21 tank cars had longitudinal tank seams and shorter, fatter tanks, as on this ICC-103 Texaco 10,000-gallon car built in 1929. *Frank Taylor*

This 6,000-gallon tank car is an ACF Type 27, a style built from 1927 through the 1940s. This general-service ICC-103 car, part of ACF's Shipper's Car Line leasing fleet, was built in 1936. *Roy C. Meates*

ACF built this insulated pressure car, a 6,000-gallon ICC-105A300 tank car, for chlorine service in 1940. Note the lip on the end (showing that it's insulated) and the small housing (instead of an expansion dome) atop the car. *ACF*

Historically, almost all revenue-service tank cars have been privately owned (96 percent in 1955). In fact, through the 1950s, there were more privately owned tank cars than all other types of privately owned car types combined. This practice dates back to the 1800s, when railroads were reluctant to invest in cars that served a single commodity or business. This left shippers and leasing companies to provide them.

Most railroad-owned tank cars are not in revenue service, but in company service (such as carrying locomotive fuel). Railroads that operated oil-fired steam locomotives tended to have fairly large fleets, notably the Santa Fe and Southern Pacific, each of which rostered more than 2,500 tank cars in the steam era.

The dominant operator of tank cars through the transition era was Union Tank Line (cars with UTLX reporting marks), which traces its history back to the Standard Oil Co. The familiar black cars with plain yellow lettering were staples in most freight trains of the transition era. Union designed its own tank cars but contracted with other companies to build them until 1955, when Union bought a tank company and began building its own cars.

The two major tank car builders of the time were also major leasing companies as well. General American built thousands of cars for UTLX and others, and also operated the second-largest tank car lease fleet (GATX reporting marks).

American Car & Foundry built cars for UTLX and other car operators from its own successful car designs. Its Shippers' Car Line subsidiary (SHPX reporting marks) was significant, but with a fleet much smaller than UTLX or GATX. The chart on page 61 shows major tank car owners as of 1947.

Refined petroleum products (especially gasoline, fuel oil, and butane/propane gas) dominated tank car traffic of the 1940s, witnessed by the many oil companies that owned their own car fleets. Through the 1950s, pipelines and trucks began taking more of this traffic off the rails.

Many types of chemicals were also carried by tank cars, and this traffic grew with the petrochemical, rubber, and plastics industries from the 1940s into the 1950s.

Tank design

By the 1920s, basic tank car construction had evolved to a point where it would remain (with some upgrades) into the 1940s. The tank itself was made by riveting together sheets of steel into a cylinder. Early tank cars had a series of radial courses, with a longitudinal bottom section that ran the length of the tank. Later tanks were formed from three or four longitudinal sections riveted together. The tank cylinder was then riveted to a stamped end.

A dome at the top of the tank allowed for load expansion, and also included a manway (with manway cover) and safety vent. Early cars had vents mounted to the side of the dome; after the early '20s, these were moved to the top of the dome.

High-pressure tanks were used for products such as propane, chlorine, and anhydrous ammonia, which are gases at normal temperature but can be liquefied under pressure and thus made more economical to transport. Relatively rare into the late 1930s, these tank cars featured thicker shells and welded construction.

These pressure tank cars were initially forge-welded, with the edges of mating steel sheets heated and hammered together. Fusion welding (such as acetylene gas or arc welding) became the norm from the mid-1930s onward. For fusion welding to work, carbuilders acquired ovens large enough to hold entire tanks to allow for the required annealing to relieve the stresses caused by the local heating of the fusion-welding process. Most non-pressure tanks continued to be riveted through the late 1940s.

Tank size varied by length and diameter. Common sizes through the transition era were nominal 8,000-, 10,000-, and 12,000-gallon cars, with larger and smaller cars for special service. Weight capacity was generally 40 tons for 8,000-gallon and smaller cars, and 50 tons for larger cars.

General American's tank cars, like this Type 30, didn't have side or end sills like ACF cars, making the bolster ends visible. This 10,000-gallon ICC-103 car was built in 1941. *Ron Stuckey, collection of John Fuller*

The mainstay of Union Tank Car's fleet was the X-3, which was the most common tank car of the transition era. This is a 10,000-gallon version of the car. *Cornelius W. Hauck*

The Illinois Railway Museum restored this 1937 UTLX short 8,000-gallon X-3 car built by ACF. Note the large platform extending past the tank end to the end sill.

Union's large 12,500-gallon X-3s can be identified by their four longitudinal tank courses, compared to three on other cars (the horizontal seam runs just below the dome platform). This one was built by ACF in 1930. *Richard H. Hendrickson*

General American built this insulated pressure car in 1940 for carrying anhydrous ammonia. It does not have side or end sills. Note the numerous chalk markings. *G. W. Sisk, collection of Jay Williams/Big Four Graphics*

This 8,000-gallon Warren car is an insulated, non-pressure car (ICC-104) built in 1927. Warren operated a large fleet of cars through the 1950s. *Trains magazine collection*

The size differences were a combination of load size needed by customers and the relative weight differences among products. Commodities varied widely in density. On the heavy side are sulfuric acid at 15 pounds per gallon and chlorine at 12.5 pounds; on the lighter side are gasoline (6 pounds per gallon) and propane (4.6 pounds).

This explains why, although chlorine and propane require similar types of cars, chlorine cars of the era were much smaller (6,000 gallons) compared to propane cars (10,500 to 11,000 gallons).

Car construction

Into the 1950s, tank cars had separate steel underframes, with center sills that ran from bolster to bolster. Above each bolster, a curved saddle cradled the tank. The tank was not anchored to the saddle. Instead, wood blocks between the steel cradle and tank allowed expansion and contraction of the tank and underframe.

Narrow steel tank bands (two or four) wrapped from the frame around the tank to secure it to the frame. These connected turnbuckle-style to the frame above each bolster and to the underframe if bands were used on either side of the dome.

Brake gear was attached to the underframe, including the control valve, cylinder, and reservoir. This equipment, along with the train line and brake rods, was generally quite visible on tank cars.

Wood running boards ran along the sides and ends of the car. (These switched to steel in the mid-1940s.) A handrail ran horizontally around the entire car as well, generally anchored to the tank on each end and to the tank or tank bands along the sides. A ladder on one or both car sides dropped down from the handrail to the running board.

Depending upon the manufacturer, some cars had end sills and brief side sills from the bolster to the end of the car; on other cars, this area was open.

The dome platform was built to the preference of the owner or lessor. Most cars had a simple dome platform of a horizontal board or steel grate above

AAR car codes for tank cars		
Class T (Tank cars*)		
TM	General-service, unlined, non-insulated car	
TA	Acid-service car (no bottom outlet)	
TL	Car equipped with special lining	
TG	Glass-lined car	
TP	Pressure tank car	
TW	Car with one or more wooden or metal tanks or tubs	
* An I suffix with any of these cars indicates an insulated car		

Cars equipped with steam coils have a pair of capped outlets for connecting to a stationary steam source.

the ladder and below the dome. Other cars had a full platform around the dome, with a low railing around the platform and gaps for ladder access.

Variations

Because they carry a tremendous variety of products, tank cars were built to multiple classifications by type of service. During the transition era, tank cars followed the Interstate Commerce Commission's (ICC) tank car classifications, which took effect for cars built in 1927 and after. The most common number classifications were 103 (a general-purpose, non-pressure car), 104 (insulated non-pressure car), and 105 (insulated, high-pressure, welded car).

Additional suffixes included A for acid service, AL for aluminum tank, C for corrosion resistant, and W for welded. Pressure cars had a number suffix to indicate the allowed pressure. Along with the ICC designations were car classes from the American Association of Railroads (AAR).

Tanks can be insulated or non-insulated. Insulated tanks were wrapped with cork or other material (foam in later years) and then covered with a thin steel sheathing. This sheathing was apparent as it would extend over the ends and leave a visible lip. The saddles would pass through the sheathing and insulation.

Insulated and non-insulated cars can both be equipped with steam-heating coils. Heating coils or tubes are used to help viscous liquids (such as tar or

Most non-pressure tank cars (except for those in acid service) have bottom outlets, although dome connections are often used for unloading.

corn syrup) flow more easily during unloading. Steam outlets were located low on the car ends or underbody. Steam outlets were connected to stationary pipes during unloading; these outlets were capped while cars were in transit.

On non-insulated cars, steam piping was internal. On insulated cars, the piping could be internal or external, between the tank and the exterior sheathing.

Pressure cars were insulated with external sheathing. They did not have conventional expansion domes or

The expansion dome on non-pressure cars includes a manway (opening) and cover, safety vent or vents, and controls for opening the bottom outlet.
Library of Congress

59

The housing atop pressure cars includes valves and connections for unloading and loading. *Library of Congress*

Multi-compartment cars have separate head shields for each compartment, shown by the radial rivet lines between expansion domes. This UTLX X-3 car was built by ACF in 1936. *ACF*

This UTLX car had a second compartment added after it was built. The 10,000-gallon car was built by Standard Tank Car Co. in 1932. *Trains magazine collection*

bottom outlets. Instead, the cylindrical housing atop the tank contained the valves and piping required for loading and unloading. Pressure cars also did not have heating coils.

Most general-service cars have bottom outlets for unloading, which are controlled by valves in the manway. Tanks carrying acids can't have bottom outlets—all unloading is through piping in the dome. Acid and food-product cars also can't have conventional safety valves. Instead, they have frangible disks that break open if the rated pressure is exceeded.

Some tank cars were built with two or more separate compartments. On these cars, each compartment had its own expansion dome. Each compartment had its own set of head shields inside the main cylinder, which on non-insulated tanks is apparent with multiple rows of rivets showing the location of the shields on the exterior.

Original multi-compartment cars can usually be identified by having domes of equal size, which are smaller than a standard dome would be for a single-compartment car of that size. Many other cars were retrofitted later, with head shields added to form two or three compartments. These cars usually retained their original dome in the center, with smaller domes above the newly formed compartments.

Evolution

The late 1940s saw an increase in the application of welded tanks for non-pressure cars. Basic car construction remained the same, with the tank secured to a separate frame.

This changed in 1954 when Union introduced its frameless tank car: a welded car that relied on the tank itself to both carry a load and transfer the train's forces. There was no longer a center sill, as bolsters on each end were welded to the tank. All brake gear was likewise welded to the tank.

The design—dubbed by UTLX as the HD, or "hot dog," car for its rounded ends and general appearance—also eliminated the expansion dome, instead calling for a 2 percent vapor space above the car's stated gallon capacity. The

Tank cars could be built smaller than standard because of specific shippers' needs or the density of the product carried. This is a welded 4,000-gallon car (ICC-103W) built by ACF for vegetable oil service in 1949. *ACF*

smaller dome instead resembled those on pressure cars, with controls and connections for loading and unloading.

Size increases were also on the horizon. The most common tank sizes through the 1950s were 8,000 to 11,000 gallons, but in the mid-1950s, the first substantially larger tank cars appeared, spurred by the overall industry-wide movement toward 70-ton cars of all types.

American Car & Foundry (ACF) built a general-purpose, 19,000-gallon welded car in 1954. Much like Union's HD car, the ACF welded car had pronounced rounded ends, although the ACF car still had an underframe and expansion dome.

Other manufacturers shortly followed suit, and Union built its first 20,000-gallon car in 1958. Although these larger cars remained rare at the end of the transition era, they were the predecessors of the even larger cars that followed in the 1960s.

The new car designs led to new ICC designations in 1957, including ICC-111A (domeless) and ICC-112A (non-insulated, high-pressure).

Common car designs

Although a tank car was designed by the United States Railroad Administration (USRA), no cars

Tank car fleets in 1947

This chart shows major tank car owners (with more than 1,500 cars). In addition, there were hundreds of small fleets of cars (some only up to a dozen, others in the hundreds), including many smaller oil companies and chemical companies. (Check an *Official Railway Equipment Register* for the year you model for details.)

Owner	Number
Union Tank Line	38,800
General American	33,500
Shippers' Car Line	9,200
Sinclair	6,100
North American	4,500
Warren Petroleum*	4,300 (1955)
Texas Co. (Texaco)**	3,900
U.S. Dept. of Defense	3,100
Shell Oil Co.	3,000
Socony-Vacuum	2,500
Canadian General Transit	2,200
Mid-Continent Petroleum (D-X)	1,600
Gulf Oil Co.	1,500

* 1947 figures are not available

** In 1936 Texaco sold its cars to General American and leased them back (these are not included in GA total)

were ever built to that specific design. There were also no American Railway Association or AAR standards for tank cars, meaning cars were built to a variety of designs, with cars of individual builders having common detail traits.

The most common tank car of the transition era was Union's X-3. This

61

General American built this 11,000-gallon pressure car (ICC-105A-300W) for carrying liquefied petroleum gas in 1955. *J. David Ingles collection*

This Defense Plant Corp. ICC-104AW tank car is being loaded with butadiene in 1944. The 11,500-gallon car was built by ACF. *Library of Congress*

Union introduced its frameless, welded HD ("hot dog") car in 1954. The car also did away with the expansion dome for general-purpose cars. *Union Tank Car*

was Union's design for a general-purpose, non-pressure, non-insulated car, and it was built in large numbers by several manufacturers from the 1920s through the 1930s. Most remained in service through the 1960s. These cars can be spotted by their side sills covering the bolster end that extend to an end sill, underframes that extend past the tank end, and wood platforms on the ends between the bolster and end sill.

The X-3 was built with several tank sizes on a short frame (32'-2") or a long frame (37'-5"). The long frame carried 8,000- and 10,000-gallon tanks (tanks 6'-4" or 8'-7" in diameter), and the short frame carried 6,500- and 8,000-gallon tanks (tanks 6'-4" or 8'-7" in diameter). The 10,000-gallon and larger cars had 50-ton capacity, with smaller cars having a 40-ton capacity. There was also a 12,500-gallon version, identified by its four longitudinal tank courses, compared to three for smaller tanks.

Union also operated the X-4, which was an insulated version of the X-3, and the X-5, an insulated pressurized car. Most Union-designed UTLX cars of this period had their design specification stenciled on the middle of each end.

American Car & Foundry built a large number of cars to its own designs. The company designated its designs by the year they were developed. The two most common ACF cars in service in the 1940s and '50s were the non-pressure, non-insulated Type 21 and Type 27 cars.

The main spotting feature of Type 21s, built from 1921 through the 1920s, was their shorter, fatter tanks compared to the later Type 27s. The Type 21s had channel-section end sills and stub side sills, visible from the bolster to each end of the car. The most common sizes were 8,000 gallons and 10,000 gallons, with the smaller versions slightly more popular.

ACF's earlier Type 17 tanks (many of which lasted through the 1940s, see page 55) can be spotted by their radial courses atop a longitudinal bottom course. The Type 21's 8,000-gallon tanks and late-production (after 1925) 10,000-gallon tanks had three longitudinal courses, and the early 10,000-gallon tanks had four courses. They had four tank bands: above each bolster and on either side of the dome.

These cars were built with KC brakes, and many had archbar or Andrews trucks, which were upgraded over the years as that equipment was banned for interchange service.

The Type 27, introduced in 1927, had the same basic appearance but with longer, narrower tanks. Early Type 27s had tanks secured by four tank bands, but the middle two were eliminated in the early 1930s. The 8,000- and 10,000-gallon versions were the most common, but 12,000-gallon cars as well as cars as small as 4,000 gallons were also built. The 8,000- and 10,000-gallon cars were 36 feet long, while the 12,000-gallon car was 39 feet long, and the 6,000-gallon car was 32 feet long. These riveted cars were built into the late 1940s, when welded cars took over.

ACF also built Type 27 pressure cars (ICC-105W), beginning in the 1930s but expanding production significantly in the 1940s. Most were 10,500- and 11,000-gallon cars, but some 3,000- and 6,000-gallon cars were built. The underframes were the same style as the non-pressure cars.

The tank for the 11,000-gallon car was slightly longer than the 10,500-gallon car, resulting in a 2-foot longer frame (39 feet instead of 37). Frames on cars with smaller tanks ranged from 32 to 36 feet long depending on the intended lading. These pressure cars were built into the 1950s, until larger cars and frameless construction took over.

The major use for pressure cars during this period was carrying propane and butane, which were taking over much of the rural home-heating fuel market from coal. Pressure cars also carried other commodities that could be liquefied under pressure, including anhydrous ammonia, butadiene, chlorine, sulfur dioxide, and tetraethyl lead.

General American's tank cars had a distinctive appearance. They didn't have end or side sills, which left the ends of bolsters visible. They had two-rung steps

Matched Santa Fe FTs lead a solid train of oil cars out of Cushing, Okla., in a scene common during World War II. *Trains magazine collection*

World War II

America's tank car fleet did yeoman duty during World War II. Tanker ships that normally carried oil from Southwest refineries to the East Coast were suddenly the targets of German U-boats; by then, most available ships were on duty carrying tremendous amounts of fuel to Great Britain.

That left railroads to carry almost all of the petroleum products and crude oil required in the country. Almost every general-purpose tank car was placed into service, and thousands of cars that had been idled in the 1930s and destined for scrapping were refurbished and returned to service. Solid trains of tank cars were operating from oilfields and refineries to both coasts. By 1943, railroads were hauling a million barrels of petroleum a day.

The completion of major pipelines by late 1943 helped ease the traffic, but solid oil trains continued to operate throughout the country until the end of the war.

Union applied its frameless design to this insulated pressure car in 1957. It's an 11,000-gallon, ICC-105A-300W car for anhydrous ammonia. *Union Tank Car*

North American introduced its Mark 20, a 100-ton, 20,000-gallon general-purpose car, in 1959. Note that it still has a frame but no expansion dome. *North American Car Corp.*

MHAX 1098, built in 1957, is one of 60 helium cars ACF built for the Department of the Interior in the late 1950s. *J. David Ingles collection*

Helium cars

Helium cars had a distinct appearance unlike any other tank car. These cars carried helium compressed to extremely high pressure (3,000–4,000 psi) in a series of thick-walled tubular tanks (30 on most cars) surrounded by a frame. Doors on the ends opened to allow access to loading/unloading valves and connectors. A total of 238 cars of this style were built from 1930 to 1962.

These cars were all operated by the U.S. Navy (USNX reporting marks) through 1955, when ownership was transferred to the Department of Interior/Bureau of Mines (MHAX reporting marks) and the Atomic Energy Commission (ATMX). Most cars operated in the transition era were built by General American (66 cars in 1942–43) and American Car & Foundry (60 cars from 1950–59).

The heavy tanks made helium cars nominal 100-ton cars, and they were indeed heavy, with a light weight of 234,000 pounds. This made them worthy of special handling in a world of 40- and 50-ton cars.

at each end of each side, and a different frame and saddle design compared to ACF cars. There were small variations during production, but the company continued building its Type 30 car (shown on page 57) through the 1940s. Significant evolutions included a move to welded underframes in 1942, followed shortly by a transition to welded tanks in the mid-1940s.

General American also built pressure cars during this period, although the company was not as prolific as ACF. The spotting features remain the same on the frame and bolsters.

Along with the major manufacturers, smaller builders included Pennsylvania Tank Car Co. (until 1929) and Standard Tank Co. Many of these cars were similar to cars of the major builders. Spotting features include tank size, car length, style of the underframe, end and side sills, and ladders.

It's also worth mentioning that Union, ACF, and General American all wound up with some of each others' cars in their lease fleets, as each leasing company was continually buying smaller car fleets from private owners. Therefore, it wasn't completely unusual for a General American-built car to show up in the SHPX lease fleet or vice-versa.

CHAPTER SEVEN

Covered hoppers

Covered hoppers are the most common car type on railroads today, which makes it difficult to believe that purpose-built covered hoppers didn't appear until the 1930s. Through the 1940s, most covered hoppers were generally small specialty cars used for hauling cement, lime, sand, and other dense bulk products, but by the end of the 1950s, these cars were carrying a broad range of commodities in ever-growing cars.

An American Car & Foundry switcher readies a string of new 1,790-cubic-foot covered hoppers for the Lackawanna in June 1950. Early covered hoppers were mainly small two-bay cars designed for cement and other heavy dry bulk products. *ACF*

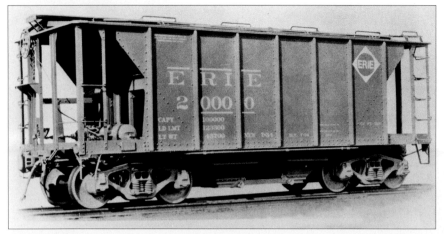

Among the first orders for purpose-built covered hoppers was a group of 50-ton, 1,321-cf cement cars built by Greenville for the Erie in 1934. *Greenville Steel Car Co.*

Pennsylvania's class H30 covered hoppers, built in 1935, had a distinctive truss-frame side and low profile. *J. David Ingles collection*

The Baltimore & Ohio had several classes of round-roof covered hoppers, including no. 630418, a 70-ton N-34 built in 1940. *Baltimore & Ohio*

Open hoppers have been used since the 1800s to haul coal, aggregates, and other bulk products that don't require protection from the elements. Dry bulk material requiring protection, such as cement, lime, foundry sand, grain, and flour, were initially packed into sacks or barrels and carried in conventional boxcars.

Into the 1900s, many of these products began to be carried in bulk in boxcars. This was fine for grain and other products that would clear a car relatively cleanly, but some products (such as cement or carbon black) would contaminate a boxcar if loaded in bulk.

The solution was putting a waterproof cover on a hopper car and adding bottom outlet gates that seal tightly even when hauling fine material. Railroads experimented with doing this in the early 1900s, and the practice became rather common through the 1920s (in fact, railroads continued the practice through the transition era).

Car manufacturers took note, and in the early 1930s, the first commercial purpose-built covered hoppers appeared. American Car & Foundry (ACF) built an experimental 70-ton, 2,050-cubic-foot (cf), 30-foot-long car in 1932. In 1934, it announced production of that car as well as a 50-ton version and a 3,000-cf, 50-ton, 40-foot car for carrying carbon black.

Among the first production cars were an order of 50 cars built by Greenville Steel Car Co. for the Erie in 1934. Designed for hauling cement, the 50-ton, 1,321-cubic-foot cars were 29 feet long and 11'-6" tall, and sported eight large square roof hatches. All were still in service in the late 1950s, showing that most early covered hoppers are very appropriate for anyone modeling part of the transition era.

These Greenville cars and other purpose-built cars differed from converted open hoppers in several features. The end slope sheets on covered hoppers angle much farther toward the roof, and usually terminate before end of the car. This is because, when loading through end hatches, it can be difficult to get product all the way to the ends under the roof.

On open hoppers, where loading at the very ends isn't a problem, the car compartment goes to the end of the body, with the slope usually starting several feet down from the top of the end.

The outlet bays and gates on covered hoppers usually have a flat bottom, and they're designed to keep fine materials from seeping out the edges of the gate. This differs from open hoppers, which usually have "saw-tooth" bays with gates at an angle.

Like open hoppers, early covered hoppers had a center sill that passed through the car. Outlet hoppers and gates are found in pairs, with one on each side of the sill. Almost all covered hoppers are designed to dump their loads between the rails.

Early cars

Along with ACF, Pullman-Standard, Greenville, and other manufacturers, many individual railroads began building covered hoppers in the 1930s. Almost all were two-bay, 50- or 70-ton cars designed for carrying cement, lime, sand, and other heavy lading, or slightly larger cars for phosphate and carbon black.

One distinctive early design was the Pennsylvania Railroad's H30 and H30A covered hopper. This car is easy to identify, with its three outlet bays and three vertical posts with angled posts coming downward from the top of each end post. This car is longer

New York Central's 70-ton Enterprise covered hoppers had diagonal braces on the end panels. This car was built in June 1940. *Trains magazine collection*

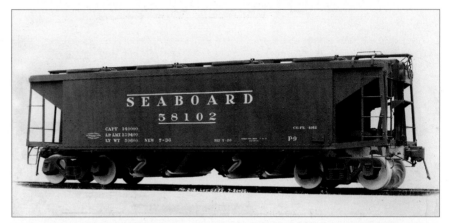

Many early larger covered hoppers, like this four-bay, 1,912-cf Seaboard Air Line car, were built for phosphate service. The 70-ton car was built in 1936. *Pullman-Standard*

(about 40 feet) and shorter in height than contemporary two-bay cars of ACF and other builders. The Pennsy built about 1,300 of these 70-ton, 1,973-cubic-foot cars from 1935 to 1946, plus another 250 nearly identical H30A cars in 1951–52.

A variation on this design is the H32, a stretched (53-foot), five-bay, 3,500-cf version of the H30. The car still had a 70-ton capacity, but it was designed for less-dense products than the smaller car. A total of 300 were built in 1948.

This three-bay ACF car was built in 1933 for carrying carbon black. The 40-ton covered hopper had a 3,000-cf capacity. *ACF*

The first common two-bay design, a 1,790-cf cement car, was designed by American Car & Foundry with the Lehigh & New England. This 70-ton car was built in 1937. *Lehigh & New England*

The 1,958-cf covered hopper became the cement car of choice in the 1940s. This 70-ton Clinchfield car was built in 1949 by ACF. *ACF*

Pullman-Standard's 1,958-cf car was nearly identical to ACF's version. This Minneapolis & St. Louis car was built in 1947. *Minneapolis & St. Louis*

The Baltimore & Ohio also built its own covered hoppers to a unique design following its successful wagontop boxcars. First built in 1935 as railroad class N-31, the 50-ton car had side sheets that wrapped around in a radius to form the roof as well. The cars had external vertical side posts, two outlet bays, and eight square roof hatches. The B&O would build three more classes of these cars (N-34, N-38, N-40) into the 1940s, upping the capacity to 70 tons.

The New York Central's Enterprise covered hoppers were another distinctive early design. They had four vertical posts with an angled post at each end. The two-bay cars with 10 roof hatches at first glance were similar to the Pennsy's cars, but the NYC cars are taller, which gives them a more conventional appearance.

The larger covered hoppers built during this time were generally designed for carrying carbon black and phosphate, less-dense products that wouldn't approach the weight limit on a smaller-volume car. Cars of various designs from ACF, Pullman-Standard, and others went to private owners and southeastern railroads (for phosphate). These cars had cubic capacities to about 3,000 cubic feet, with three or four bays and sets of outlet gates.

Design evolution

The first popular common covered-hopper design was developed in 1937 by ACF in working with the Lehigh & New England, which handled a lot of cement. The 70-ton car had a 1,790-cf capacity with 10 square (30" or 36") hatches, triangular cutaways in the sides between bays, and nine vertical side supports (C-channels on the ends with formed steel for the rest).

This soon evolved into a more popular version, a 1,958-cf car that was 3 feet longer (35'-3" compared to 32'-4") with eight roof hatches, but otherwise looked similar. The larger car would prove more versatile and more popular, and ACF built it in large numbers into the 1950s. Many cars of this same basic design were also built by Pullman-Standard, General American, and other manufacturers beginning in 1940.

Covered hoppers remained largely unchanged into the 1950s, when Pullman-Standard redesigned its cars with the introduction of the PS-2 line in 1952. They were based on the company's earlier cars, but introduced all-welded construction. The PS-2 designation covered all covered hoppers regardless of size (just as there were many variations in PS-1 boxcars). As with cars from other builders, P-S covered hoppers were labeled by their capacity in cubic feet.

The first PS-2 car was a two-bay, 2,003-cf, 70-ton covered hopper. The 30-foot car introduced circular roof hatches (30"-diameter), designed to provide a better seal than square designs, and could be spotted by its 4/4 vertical post pattern, with a gap between the posts. The end posts were initially C-channels, but around 1957, they became steel shapes to match the other posts.

Pullman-Standard soon added larger cars to the PS-2 line; popular cars were the 2,893-cf car in 1953 and the 3,219-cf (also called 3,215) car in 1958. Both were 42-foot-long, three-bay, 70-ton cars, identifiable by their 4/3/4 side post patterns. The 3,219 car is 5" taller and slightly wider than the 2,893. Both had round roof hatches with a center running board.

These longer cars found themselves in service hauling a variety of new products, including salt, corn meal, soybean meal, malted barley, fertilizer, and sugar. Although these cars carried some grain, it wasn't yet common. Covered hoppers weren't widely used for grain until the introduction of larger 100-ton cars with trough hatches, which wouldn't arrive until the early 1960s.

ACF and Greenville also revised their designs in the early 1950s by eliminating the triangular cutouts of older cars, adopting welded construction, increasing size (and offering more size options—ACF's were 2,006-cf and 2,927-cf), and moving to round hatches.

The PS-2 ushered in a new car design and welded construction from Pullman-Standard. This 2,003-cf covered hopper was built in 1957. *Pullman-Standard*

Other manufacturers, including Greenville, followed Pullman's design lead. Welded Western Maryland no. 5701 was built in 1955. *Greenville Steel Car Co.*

The Burlington built this 1,958-cf car with square roof hatches for its Colorado & Southern subsidiary in its own shops in 1958, several years after round hatches and 2,003-cf cars had become common. *J. David Ingles collection*

Pullman's 2,893-cf car was a hit when introduced in 1953. It became popular for carrying feed, fertilizer, salt, meal, and other products. This Soo Line car was built in 1957. *J. David Ingles collection*

In 1958, P-S bumped up the capacity of the three-bay PS-2 to 3,219 cubic feet. It was slightly taller than the 2,893 car but had a very similar appearance. *Chicago, Burlington & Quincy*

General American's Airslide car, introduced in 1954, had a boxy appearance and longitudinal internal hoppers, resulting in a unique outlet bay. This Burlington car was built in 1958. *Chicago, Burlington & Quincy*

Airslide cars

A successful specialized type of covered hopper, the Airslide, was introduced by General American in 1954. Unlike other covered hoppers, the bays in Airslide cars are longitudinal to the car, with steep side-to-side slopes and shallow end-to-end slopes.

What makes the Airslide design unique is that the bottom of each hopper trough is lined with special perforated fabric. During unloading, a low-pressure air supply (such as a stationary source at a loading dock or a truck) is connected to the car. The air passes through the fabric lining and effectively liquefies the lading so it flows smoothly out of the car and allows the car to empty cleanly.

This, coupled with the car's weatherproof hatches, made Airslide cars popular for carrying powdered and granular products that tended to clump in standard covered hoppers. These include feed, plastic pellets, plastic powder, carbon black, and food-grade products such as flour, sugar, and corn starch.

Airslide cars can be readily identified by their distinctive, boxy appearance without visible end slope sheets, as compared to a standard covered hopper, and their unique outlet gates.

Most Airslide cars built from 1954 into 1960 were the small (2,600-cf) single-bay version. Through this period, these cars had open framing at each end with diagonal braces from the bottoms of the ends to the top of the body, and 11 side posts (channels at each end). This car has six loading hatches (three on each side of the center running board) and was built in 50-ton and 70-ton versions.

A larger (3,600-cf) two-bay version was also built during this time. This car was longer (53 feet) with two outlet bays, 13 exterior side posts, and 10 roof hatches—five in a staggered pattern on each side of the running board. The car had the same style of open ends with bracing as the 2,600-cf car. An even larger car (4,180-cf) that eliminated the open ends would eventually

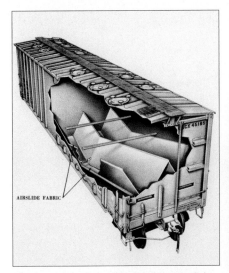

This cutaway view of a two-bay Airslide shows the longitudinal hoppers and the location of the perforated fabric. *General American*

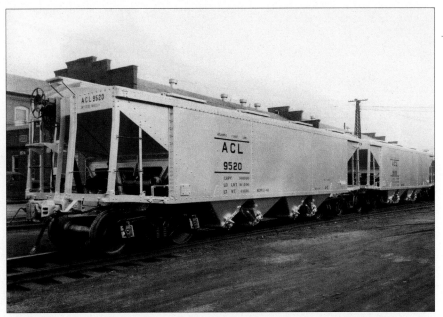

Specialized cars for phosphate continued to be built through the 1940s. The 1,970-cf, four-bay, 70-ton cars were low-slung and had a similar profile to the 1930s cars. *ACF*

become very popular, but it wasn't built until the 1960s.

Many railroads and private owners purchased Airslide cars, and General American also had them in its lease fleet (GACX reporting marks). More than 3,400 were in service by the end of 1959.

Evolution

As more commodities began traveling in covered hoppers, builders adapted by customizing them and fitted cars with special equipment including interior car linings (to offer resistance to chemicals), outlet gates, and other components.

By the late 1950s, outlet gates on covered hoppers could be gravity, pneumatic, or combination outlets. Gravity outlets were the most common. These had a plate that slid to the side to allow the load to empty.

For food-grade products and many chemicals, this posed a risk of contamination, so the pneumatic outlet was developed. These can be spotted by a pipe or pipes across the outlet bay. An unloading hose or pipe is connected, and the load is vacuumed or forced by air out of the car.

Combination outlets allow either gravity or pneumatic unloading.

Through the 1940s and 1950s, ACF and Pullman-Standard dominated the covered-hopper market, but Greenville

Railroads continued converting older open hoppers into covered hoppers through the 1950s, as shown by this Toledo, Peoria & Western car in 1960. *J. David Ingles collection*

and many smaller builders, along with several railroads in their own shops, continued to build cars. Many of these cars followed ACF and P-S designs very closely.

Spotting features to look for on covered hoppers include construction technique (welded or riveted), car length and height, cubic capacity, rib placement and style (channel or formed steel), end framing and

ladders, roof, type of outlet gates, and hatches (including size, number, and placement).

How you add these cars to your layout will be determined by the railroad and region you model, as well as the specific year modeled. During the transition era, the covered hopper went from a rare specialty car to a common bulk hauler, with about 75,000 cars in service by 1959.

CHAPTER EIGHT

Flatcars

Flatcars carry a tremendous variety of items, including piggyback trailers as seen on the Chicago & North Western in 1954. With the addition of side rails and bridge plates, this 53-foot flatcar was converted to carry trailers. *Chicago & North Western*

Since the beginning of railroading, flatcars have been employed for carrying almost any bulky item or product, including machinery, pipes, pulpwood, and lumber. Flatcars can be plain for general service or fitted with a variety of loading racks to haul anything from auto frames to containers and piggyback trailers. One of the features that makes flatcars appealing for modelers is the variety of visible loads that they carry.

By the early 1900s, most flatcars featured all-steel construction. The United States Railroad Administration (USRA) designed a 55-ton, 42-foot flatcar while it controlled U.S. railroads during World War I and the years after. Although none were actually built under USRA control, about 8,000 cars were built to the basic USRA design (or similar designs from 40–43 feet long) for several railroads through 1930. The solid construction of these cars allowed most to stay in service through the 1950s.

These cars featured riveted construction and relied on fishbelly sides, meaning for strength the middle was deeper (hung lower) than the ends, with a taper from the narrow ends to the wide middle area inside each truck.

These cars had 12 stake pockets riveted along the top of each side that could hold vertical metal or wood posts or be used to anchor chains or straps. Wood decks allowed load blocking and anchors to be easily secured to the deck.

The brake wheel was generally mounted on a vertical staff at the B end of the car. Flatcars have drop staffs, which allow the wheel and staff to be lowered so the wheel is just below floor level to clear loads.

Design evolution

By the late 1920s, railroads were finding that longer flatcars provided more versatility. Most cars built from the late 1920s onward were longer, with some 46-foot cars and several in the 50- to 53-foot range.

This led to the American Association of Railroads (AAR) in 1941 recommending a trio of nominal 50-foot designs. The 50-ton, 53'-6" AAR riveted design was based on a Union Pacific car built by Pullman-Standard (class F-50-11). The car had fishbelly sides with a single taper and 15 stake pockets on each side (with the middle stake slightly to the right of center on each side). A similar 70-ton car was based on an Erie car built by Pressed Steel Car Co. Cars were built to these designs through the 1950s.

A third design featured a 70-ton, 50-foot car with a cast underframe, patterned after the Pennsylvania Railroad's F30A car. Although this

This 42-foot Detroit, Toledo & Ironton flatcar, built in 1925, follows the lines of USRA-design cars. Rails on the deck allow it to carry rail wheelsets. *J. David Ingles collection*

Most flatcars have brakewheels on drop staffs, allowing them to rest below the deck surface. This is a late-1950s Pullman-Standard car. *Pullman-Standard*

This 53-foot Union Pacific car, built in the railroad's Omaha shops in 1939, was converted to piggyback service by 1954. The bridge plates are down and the trailers chained to the side rails. *Union Pacific*

The Pennsy built just over 2,000 versions of its F30 cast-underframe flatcar. This is an F30E car built in 1954. *Pennsylvania Railroad*

One of the most common flatcars of the 1950s was the 53-foot GSC Commonwealth car. The entire body was a single casting. The GSC bulkheads were a customer option. *Union Pacific*

Some flats, like this Burlington car, had straight sides. For strength, these cars had deeper center sills (its shadow can be seen under the car). The wood blocking for the load is nailed to the deck. *J. David Ingles collection*

design wasn't popular (other than with the Pennsy), it led to one of the most popular flatcars of the 1950s and 1960s, the Commonwealth flatcar.

General Steel Castings (GSC), which made the cast underframes for the Pennsy F30, stretched the design to 53'-6" and made the entire body a single casting. The resulting car, which debuted in the early 1950s, was initially sold as a kit to railroads and later offered as a complete car.

Commonwealth flatcars are identifiable by their unique multi-taper fishbelly sides that angle more sharply near the trucks and then step down before reaching the horizontal portion, as well as their lack of rivets and their stake pockets, which are cast integral to the car.

These cars could be found equipped for a variety of services, with bulkheads (either GSC's own open-lattice cast-steel designs, which were made in several heights, or others) or many types of loading racks. The same basic design was offered into the 1960s.

Flatcars were built to other designs before and during this period. Probably the best spotting feature for a flatcar is the sides. Cars have either a fishbelly shape (most common during the transition era)—along with the shape of the taper—or a straight sill. Cars with straight side sills have a heavier center sill, which is usually noticeable when viewing the car from the side.

The number and type of stake pockets is also a spotting feature. Pockets can be cast or stamped, and they can be spaced evenly or unevenly across the top of the sides.

Other things to look for include whether a car has riveted or welded (more common after 1950) construction, the type of brake wheel and its location, the type of trucks, and special equipment such as loading racks, bulkheads, or piggyback (trailer) equipment.

Bulkheads and racks

Railroads equipped some flatcars with bulkheads—walls at each end of the car—to better carry loads that required support or that could shift with slack action, including lumber and pulpwood. Bulkheads varied in height depending upon their intended service. They could be furnished new with the car, or added later by the railroad.

Loading racks of many types were added to flatcars. These were custom built to fit specific loads, such as auto frames, shipping containers, steel beams and components, railcar wheelsets, machinery, and tractors (or other non-automobile vehicles). Cars like this would generally be in dedicated service for a specific customer.

Automobile-loading racks began appearing at the end of the transition

Flexivan cars

An attempt at a dedicated trailer/car system for the growing piggyback market was the Flexi-Van, a venture between the New York Central and trailer/container manufacturer Strick. Flexi-Van containers had separate highway wheel assemblies (bogies), as opposed to today's containers, which have wheels on a chassis that runs under the entire container. Flexi-Van 85-foot flatcars had a heavy center spine. Instead of a full deck, each car had a pair of rotating turntables, one for each container.

The cars were loaded from the side. A tractor would back the trailer to the turntable on the flatcar. As the trailer slid onto the turntable, the bogie would be unlocked and the body continued until it was centered and locked on the turntable. The container was then rotated and locked to the car.

The system, introduced in 1957, was fairly successful. The NYC ran Flexi-Van service

A truck shoves a Flexi-Van into position onto a turntable on one of the system's special spine cars, each of which holds two 40-foot containers. *New York Central*

on many routes of its system, and continued upgrading cars and containers through the 1960s. Railroads including the Chicago, Burlington & Quincy, Illinois Central, Milwaukee Road, and others also bought and operated equipment, but not until the 1960s.

era. By the mid-1950s, railroads were losing a lot of their finished-auto traffic to trucks. In an effort to regain this business, railroads tried mounting large racks atop conventional flatcars.

The first attempt, in 1954, was the Evans Auto Loader, which held six cars. An experiment of the New York Central and Evans, the loader was an evolution of Evans' boxcar auto-rack loading system adapted to a flatcar.

Although loading and unloading went quicker than with boxcars, the process was still somewhat cumbersome. A built-in ramp on the upper level hinged downward, matching another lower ramp that moved upward, allowing autos to be driven up the ramp. Only one car was ever built (although the car has been produced in model form in various scales), and the design did not prove successful.

In the meantime, by the late 1950s, with the success and growth of trailer-on-flatcar operations, several railroads began hauling auto-carrier trailers as flatcar loads. Although the system worked, railroads continued to look for methods to place more autos on a single railcar with easy loading and unloading.

The idea that would prove successful was the multilevel rack with fixed levels, allowing autos to be driven up a stationary end ramp and, as with piggyback trailers, driven down any number of railcars for loading.

This ACF 50-ton, 53-foot car was built in 1951. The vertical posts are held by steel cradles that sit on the deck under the logs. *L. E. Shawver*

Lumber was often carried on general-purpose flats through the 1950s. The vertical boards are held by the stake pockets. *Harold Hill*

A pair of new Railway Express Agency delivery trucks are themselves being delivered on a 50-foot Seaboard flatcar in 1958. The flatcar was built in 1940. *J. David Ingles collection*

This 53-foot Rock Island bulkhead car, built in 1951, had loading cables added in the late 1950s to carry small containers. *J. David Ingles collection*

In 1954, an early experiment at hauling autos on flatcar racks was the Evans Auto-Loader, which held six autos on a 53-foot flat. No other examples were built. *New York Central*

The system was first tried on shorter cars, as shown on the Santa Fe car on the opposite page, but it would flourish with the long auto racks that would soon be installed atop the 85-foot piggyback flatcars that began appearing in 1958. This large-scale auto-rack traffic wouldn't get rolling until 1960, at the very end of the transition era.

Piggyback flatcars

By 1940, several railroads were offering trailer-on-flatcar (TOFC, or piggyback) service, either with their own trailers or—in a few cases—hauling commercial carriers' trailers. Piggyback service at the time was labor-intensive. All cars were loaded and unloaded "elephant style" at ramps, with tractors backing trailers into position, possibly along a string of several cars.

Flatcars had to be specially equipped for TOFC service. Railroads would adapt a variety of cars for this, including some older 40-foot cars as well as newer 53-foot cars. Most were set up to carry a single trailer, but 53-foot cars were sometimes equipped to carry a pair of 20-foot trailers.

Each car had a hinged fold-down bridge plate at each end to enable trailers to cross between cars. If you're standing on the ground looking at the end of the car, this plate is on the right.

Cars had raised rub rails along the edge of the deck on each side to keep trailer wheels from going over the edge when loading. Collapsible hitches hadn't yet been invented, so cars had large jacks or stands to hold up the kingpin end of a trailer, along with several chains and tie-down hooks or rails.

Trailer loading was cumbersome. Once a trailer was backed into position, the jack was placed under the kingpin and a series of chains—up to 40 in some cases—were connected and tightened to secure the trailer.

Because each railroad used its own flatcars and had its own system of tying down trailers, most piggyback operations into the mid-1950s were intraline, with equipment rarely straying off-line.

Several attempts were made to standardize piggyback equipment

AAR car codes for flatcars	
Class F (Flatcars)	
FM	General-service car
FC	Piggyback car
FD	Depressed-center car
FB	Barrel-rack car (skeleton car)
FL	Logging car

The Santa Fe tried this three-level rack, which could hold nine cars, in 1960, just as the transition era was closing. *Ford Motor Co.*

The Minneapolis & St. Louis converted this 50-foot flatcar, built in 1931, to piggyback service in the 1950s. Old rails were popular to use as both rub rails and anchors for chains. *J. David Ingles Collection*

Trailer Train's 75-foot F39 cars were rendered obsolete soon after being built by the coming of 40-foot trailers, such as this Norfolk & Western example in 1959. *J. David Ingles collection*

and speed the loading and unloading process. The most influential of these came in 1955 with the development of the American Car & Foundry (ACF) Model A trailer hitch. The device, anchored to a flatcar bed, could be raised and lowered by a power wrench. It locked to the trailer kingpin and eliminated the need for other tie-down equipment. It saved a great deal of time and labor, and made interchange of piggyback cars much more practical.

The new trailer hitch, along with some Interstate Commerce Commission rulings, led to a surge in piggyback traffic from the mid-1950s onward. In 1955, railroads loaded a total of 168,000 piggyback flats; by 1958, it was 278,000; and by 1960, it was 554,000.

Into the mid-1950s, piggyback flatcars were all existing cars that had been fitted with the necessary equipment. The first flats built specifically to haul trailers without modification were 500 (class F39) 75-foot cars built by and for the Pennsylvania Railroad in 1955. The F39s were built with Model A hitches and were designed to carry a pair of trailers up to 35 feet in length, the longest trailers in service at the time. They were distinctive by their length and their rub rail/tie-down rails along their sides.

These cars were transferred to Trailer Train (TTX reporting marks) when that consortium was formed in late 1955. Trailer Train, formed initially by the Pennsylvania and Norfolk & Western railroads, provided a pool of piggyback equipment that could be shared by member railroads. The concept was a success; by 1959, 19 railroads had joined, and in 1960, 32 railroads were members.

In 1957, 40-foot semi trailers became legal across the country,

The ACF Model A trailer hitch revolutionized piggyback traffic. A power wrench was used to lock the jaw to the trailer kingpin as well as raise and lower the hitch to floor level.

Longer piggyback flatcars began to appear in the late 1950s. This 88-foot flat holds two Santa Fe 40-foot trailers. The flatcar still uses outdated jacks instead of a trailer hitch. *Santa Fe*

This depressed-center car, built in 1957, rides on a pair of six-wheel roller-bearing trucks. The car has a load limit of 251,000 pounds. *Chicago & Eastern Illinois*

The casting riding on this car weighs 292,700 pounds—under the car's 333,000-pound load limit. Each end of the car, built in 1951, sits on a span bolster over a pair of four-wheel trucks. *Pennsylvania Railroad*

essentially making the 75-foot cars obsolete. Trailer Train responded by developing specifications for 85-foot cars, with the first 800 arriving in 1958. By 1960, Trailer Train had several thousand 85-foot flatcars in service.

During this time, many individual railroads continued to operate piggyback flatcars (see the Santa Fe car above), but cars with TTX reporting marks had began taking their dominant place on the rails.

Heavy-duty flatcars

Heavy-capacity flatcars are used for some of the heaviest and bulkiest loads that travel on railroads, items such as large electrical transformers, generators, turbines, and boilers. Some of these specialized cars have flat decks like a standard flatcar, but to provide extra clearance, most are depressed-center cars, with the area between trucks lowered.

These cars have tonnage ratings well above those of standard freight cars, to 200 tons and even higher in some cases. To handle these heavy loads, most cars above a 100-ton rating have special (six-wheel) trucks or bolsters that span a pair of trucks (four-, six-, or even eight-wheel) above each end of a car to better spread the weight.

Most railroads had a handful of these cars, but some railroads had more, especially if they had on-line customers who made frequent use of them. For example, the Pennsylvania Railroad in 1955 had about 225 cars classified as heavy-capacity flatcars.

These cars were built to a number of designs over the years. Spotting features include trucks, car length, depth of the sides, shape of the bed (on depressed-center cars), and design of the ends and how they mount to the trucks.

Large loads moved on these cars are almost always treated as special movements. You won't see one of these loaded cars doing 60 mph in a merchandise freight train. Instead, the car will likely be treated as a train by itself, with a locomotive separated from the flatcar by one or more idler (empty) cars to spread the weight on bridges. Routes for these loaded cars are carefully planned, both for vertical and horizontal clearance as well as for weight.

CHAPTER NINE

Stock cars

Shipping livestock by rail was common through the transition era. Livestock traffic was on the downswing by the 1950s, but plenty of stock cars were in use through the decade.

Unlike the trend toward steel construction in other car types by the 1930s, stock cars relied on wood construction (with steel underframes) into the 1950s. Older cars featuring outdated designs with wood roofs and ends, as well as shorter cars (36-foot-long), remained in service through the transition era. Cars with 30- and 40-ton capacities were common late in stock car operations. Stock cars were often shorter in height compared to boxcars, commonly 8 or 9 feet (inside height) compared to 10'-0" to 10'-6" for boxcars.

This 1955 view along the Chicago, Burlington & Quincy highlights how car construction evolved over 27 years. The car at left is a 36-foot, steel-underframe car with wood ends and roof built by American Car & Foundry (ACF) in 1922. The car at right, built in Burlington's Havelock shops in 1949, is a 40-footer with steel Dreadnaught ends and panel roof. *William A. Akin*

Mather cars have wood bodies with a unique bracing pattern, and they used common steel shaped for bracing. This is a 40-foot car; early Mather cars were 36 feet long. *Donald Sims*

This 40-foot Southern Railway car has wood ends, metal truss side bracing with wood slats, and a wood roof. It was built by Ralston Steel Car Co. in 1939. *Ralston Steel Car Co.*

The Illinois Railway Museum restored this Santa Fe single-deck stock car. It's from Class SK-T, a 40-foot car built in 1929.

Part of this practice was expense-related. Railroads had always been reluctant to invest heavily in specialty cars such as stock cars. Livestock traffic was largely seasonal, peaking in the fall, and railroads didn't want to invest money in new cars that stood idle much of the year. They instead upgraded, repaired, and rebuilt cars as needed each year.

Another factor was the decline in livestock traffic by World War II. More and more livestock began traveling by truck in the 1930s, and the total number of stock cars in service declined from then through the 1950s (from 97,000 cars in 1932 to 54,000 in 1941 and 31,000 by 1960). This meant that railroads didn't have to order or build many new cars (from 1932 to 1942, only 2,300 new stock cars were built), and they could retire older cars requiring major repairs.

Car strength was also a factor. Stock cars didn't need particularly strong construction. Cattle loads didn't exceed weight limits (even a full load of grown steers would just approach the limit for a 30-ton car), and stock cars (unlike boxcars or reefers) didn't have to be weathertight—if an older wood roof leaked a bit, it was no big deal.

All of these factors led to a large variety in car styles, construction, and designs, with stock cars being built in relatively small lots compared to other freight cars.

Most Class 1 railroads operated some stock cars, but the major owners were centered in the territories where the most livestock was raised. The Santa Fe operated the most cars, followed by the Union Pacific and other western railroads. Among eastern roads, the Pennsy and New York Central operated relatively large fleets of stock cars, mainly because of their position in carrying livestock from the huge Chicago Union Stock Yards to New York City.

In addition, several private owners and leasing companies operated their own smaller car fleets, including Mather Car Co. (950 cars in 1943) and Quaker Livestock Express (500 cars in 1943). Packing companies Armour had 200 cars and Swift had 860 cars.

Single- and double-deck cars

Stock cars fell into three main classifications: single-deck (AAR class SM), double-deck (SF), and convertible double-deck (SC).

Single-deck cars were used primarily for steers and other cattle that were too large to travel in two-deck cars. Double-deck cars had a fixed upper floor. These were used for smaller animals, mainly hogs and sheep. Double-deck cars required special loading ramps (either fixed or portable) that allowed animals to get to the upper level.

Many double-deck cars had separate half-height doors for each deck, although some had a single door. The ends of the boards for the upper deck can often be seen through the side slats on double-deck cars, or there will be an extra slat at the location of the deck.

Convertible cars had an upper deck that could either be removed from the car or stored at ceiling level when not in use. These could be lowered into position for hauling hogs or sheep. These would have a visible mechanism, with cables and a crank for moving the upper deck. This mechanism would only be on one side of the car.

Common designs

There was no United States Railroad Administration (USRA) stock car design as with boxcars and other cars, so stock cars were built to many unique designs. The first attempt at standardizing a stock car came in 1927, with discussions resulting in 1930 American Railway Association (ARA) designs for 40-foot, 40- and 50-ton cars. These were approved as recommended practice (but not as a standard). These designs called for steel-underframe cars with wood ends, steel truss side framing with slatted wood sides, and a steel-over-wood roof.

Stock cars were built by several railroads in their own shops and by all the major car builders, as well as many smaller builders such as Pressed Steel Car Co., Pennsylvania Car Co., Ralston Steel Car Co., and Ryan Car Co.

As cars were built, manufacturers (and railroads for homebuilt cars) typically updated their designs based on components and designs for contemporary boxcars. These included

Major stock car owners			
Railroads owning at least 1,000 stock cars in 1943			
Railroad	1943	1950	1955
Santa Fe	7,900	7,300	7,700
Union Pacific	6,000	4,500	3,300
Chicago & North Western	4,600	3,800	2,100
Southern Pacific	4,700	3,100	2,300
Milwaukee Road	3,900	3,700	3,300
Burlington Route	3,500	3,600	3,500
Canadian National	3,000	3,000	2,900
Canadian Pacific	2,700	3,400	2,800
Pennsylvania	2,400	2,400	1,300
Great Northern	1,900	2,000	1,700
Northern Pacific	1,800	1,700	1,700
Rock Island	1,500	1,200	800
New York Central	1,400	1,700	1,600
Missouri Pacific	1,400	1,500	1,500
Baltimore & Ohio	1,200	1,200	900
Illinois Central	1,200	1,100	700
Rio Grande	1,100	1,300	900

This ACF-built, 40-foot car is one of 100 built for Missouri Pacific subsidiary International-Great Northern in 1940. It has steel Dreadnaught ends. *ACF*

steel Dreadnaught ends and panel roofs in the 1930s.

Rebuilt cars don't show up in the tallies of new cars mentioned here, but this is how many railroads acquired what were essentially new cars from the 1930s through the 1940s.

Boxcars in need of major repair were a prime starting point for these rebuilds, and among the most common were USRA single- and double-sheathed boxcars and other early steel-underframe cars of the 1910s and '20s.

You can spot the heritage of many rebuilt cars. Cars rebuilt from single-

sheathed cars typically kept their steel framing, retaining the same pattern, and kept their steel ends (Murphy or Dreadnaught). Stock cars rebuilt from double-sheathed boxcars can be spotted by the fishbelly center sill of those cars.

These rebuilds tend to stand out because of their height, standing taller than earlier stock cars. They kept their original ends, which dictated the height of the car.

Spotting features of stock cars include car length and height, roof (wood or steel of different types), and ends (wood with various bracing

Burlington no. 58214 is a double-deck, 36-foot car (with single door) built in 1924, one of 1,500 in its class. The ends of the upper-deck boards are visible through the slats. *Collection of Jay Williams/Big Four Graphics*

This Southern Pacific class S-40-5 car, built in 1917, was one of thousands of similar "Harriman" cars operated by the SP and subsidiaries as well as Union Pacific. *Ralston Car Co.*

The New York Central rebuilt this stock car from a USRA boxcar in 1948—a giveaway is the 5/5/5 Murphy end. The double-deck car has separate doors for each deck. *New York Central*

patterns, Murphy steel, Dreadnaught steel of different patterns).

The side truss design is also important in the number of panels, the direction of the angles, and the truss components themselves (stamped-metal/hat-shaped, steel channel, L-shaped, Z-shaped). Wood slats were used into the mid-1950s, when some new and rebuilt cars began receiving steel slats. Lettering boards of various sizes and shapes, over the trusses, are another side detail.

Other details to look for are the sideframe, underframe, running board, doors, and ladders and grab irons. As with other freight cars, trucks and brake gear also vary. Many stock cars rode on older-style trucks to the point that they became illegal for interchange.

One common stock car design through the 1940s was the Mather car. Mather built, sold, and leased boxcars, reefers, and stock cars that all featured simple construction using stock building materials, with as few commercial or specialty parts as possible, to keep costs down.

On Mather stock cars, this meant using wood ends and roofs and basic steel shapes for bracing. They can easily be spotted by their side trusses, which had U-channel diagonals and Z-shaped vertical posts, with a pair of flat, metal diagonal straps on the end panel of each side.

Mather cars built into the 1930s were 36 feet long, while later cars were 40 feet long. In the late 1950s, Mather produced a 50-foot car by combining two rebuilt 40-foot cars. These cars were distinctive, as few 50-foot stock cars were ever built. They retained their other spotting features, and they were double-deck cars, with pairs of side-by-side doors (separate upper and lower) on each side.

Mather leased some cars to railroads and private operators through the 1950s, and other railroads purchased Mather cars outright. Cars on long-term leases were generally painted in the lessor railroad's own paint scheme and carried the railroad's reporting marks and numbers. Cars on short-term lease retained Mather (MSCX) reporting marks.

AAR car codes for stock cars	
Class S (Stock cars)	
SM	Single-deck car
SF	Double-deck car
SC	Convertible double-deck car
SD	Car with drop-bottom doors
SH	Horse car
SP	Poultry car

The Chicago & North Western rebuilt 900 stock cars from old boxcars in 1954 and 1955. They inaugurated the road's green-and-yellow scheme. *Lloyd Keyser*

Pennsy rebuilt several classes of old round-roof boxcars into stock cars, including this class K11 car with its unique rectangular screened openings. *J. David Ingles collection*

The Union Pacific also rebuilt boxcars into stock cars, using single-sheathed auto boxcars to make its class S-40-10 cars with Murphy ends. *J. David Ingles collection*

Another common design into the 1940s were Harriman cars, which were found in large numbers on the Southern Pacific and the Union Pacific with lesser numbers on the Western Pacific. The UP bought about 2,500 class S-40-4 cars and another 1,000 similar S-40-6 cars from 1912 to 1918. SP bought just over 2,800 Harriman cars in five classes from 1912 through 1927, and the WP acquired almost 200 similar cars from 1924 to 1927.

Harriman cars were 36 feet long, with steel underframes (Bettendorf steel center sills), channel-steel side sills, and wood ends and a roof. On each side, there were three panels on each side of the door. From the door outward, the first two diagonals go from bottom to top, with the last from top to bottom.

A majority survived in nearly as-built condition through the 1940s, albeit with upgrades to brake gear and trucks, and some made it through the 1950s.

Late cars

By the late 1940s, railroads were trying to figure out how to reclaim the livestock traffic that was moving to trucks. High-speed trains and car upgrades were two things tried by some railroads.

In 1947, the Union Pacific inaugurated the *Daylight Livestock* (DLS), a new high-speed stock train that ran between Salt Lake City and Los Angeles. To increase train speed and reliability and to provide a smoother ride (to lower cattle injuries and resulting claims), the UP upgraded 800 older stock cars for this service. Improvements included new, smooth slats, cushioned draft gear, and roller-bearing trucks—among the first uses of roller bearings on standard freight cars. The UP also gave these cars a new paint

scheme, yellow sides (compared to the standard red), and aluminum roofs and ends to better reflect the hot desert sun.

The original American Railway Association design was revised in 1951 by the American Association of Railroads (AAR) to reflect design improvements, with drawings calling

for a diagonal-panel roof and improved Dreadnaught ends (based on the Union Pacific's S-40-15 car), but by then, few new stock cars were being built. Railroads ordered 500 new stock cars in 1950 and 1,000 in 1951, but that was all through the 1950s (other than 400 cars in 1955).

The Union Pacific also rebuilt boxcars into double-deck cars, as with this S-40-13 car, in 1952. Note the three panels on each side of the door, compared to four on the S-40-10 car. *J. David Ingles collection*

Northern Pacific rebuilt several old 40-foot boxcars into all-steel "Pig Palace" double-deck cars in 1958. The cars had adjustable steel slats. *Northern Pacific*

North American, which owned Mather in the 1950s, rebuilt pairs of 40-foot Mather stock cars into new 50-foot, double-deck stock cars, which had two sets of doors. *J. David Ingles collection*

Wood slats deteriorate and are more easily damaged, leaving jagged splits that could injure animals. The Union Pacific began rebuilding cars with steel slats in the mid-1950s. Steel slats were thought to transfer heat too readily and cause burns on animals, but this proved to not be the case.

Northern Pacific rebuilt 200 older boxcars into double-deck stock cars in 1958, upgrading them and dubbing them "Pig Palace" cars. Innovations included all-steel sides (including slats), moveable slats so that openings could be closed in cold weather, cushioned draft gear, and roller-bearing trucks.

Although other innovations—including 86-foot cars—would arrive in the 1960s, the traffic loss could not be stopped, and the era of shipping livestock by rail was in its twilight as the transition era closed.

Poultry cars

Poultry cars were a distinctive type of stock car (AAR class SP). They represented a very small share of all stock cars: around 2,800 cars in 1932, but down to around 400 by the early 1940s. They were mainly used on the East Coast, carrying birds to New York City and other large markets.

Poultry cars varied slightly among builders, but they all had a series of racks to hold individual cages of live birds (mainly turkeys and chickens). The screened-mesh sides provided an open view of the birds on loaded cars.

The center of each car was enclosed, providing room for an attendant, who rode with the car in transit and fed and watered the birds. The enclosed area included a bunk, stove, and sink, as well as access to an onboard water tank and feed bin.

Almost all poultry cars were privately owned. North American became the dominant owner of these cars by the 1930s by acquiring the Palace Poultry Car Co. and the Live Poultry Transit Co. In 1944, North American spun off the remaining 400 or so cars to the Poultry Transit Co. (PTC). As poultry traffic shifted to trucks, the need for poultry cars continued declining until PTC went out of business in 1956.

CHAPTER TEN

Trucks and brake gear

Trucks, wheels, couplers, and brake gear are common components on all freight cars. All evolved through the transition era, and knowing how these components work and being able to spot differences among the various types will help you build and choose more realistic models based on the specific period you model.

The AAR solid-bearing truck was the mainstay of the transition era, but they were not all the same—there was a tremendous variety in styles. This is a Gould double-truss, plankless truck. Raised lettering on the sideframe truck lists the manufacturer and type, the date built (7-49), that it's an AAR design, and the initials of the Delaware, Lackawanna & Western. It was installed new on an American Car & Foundry covered hopper for the DL&W that year. *Trains magazine collection*

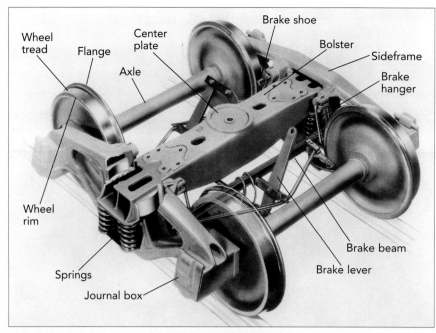

This drawing shows a spring-plankless, double-truss truck. *Buckeye Steel Castings*

The Bettendorf T-section truss was the first cast truck with journal boxes cast integral to the sideframe. *Trains magazine collection*

This AAR U-section truck was built by Bettendorf. It has a spring plank (the channel the springs rest upon) that extends between sideframes.

Trucks

The truck is the assembly under each end of a car that holds the wheels and enables the car to ride on the tracks. Truck design and construction evolved a great deal from the 1920s through the 1950s, with various types being introduced and becoming obsolete over the years.

Almost all freight-car trucks have two axles and four wheels. The trucks are not solidly attached to a freight car. Instead, gravity does the work of holding the car in place, with a kingpin at the center of each car bolster fitting into holes on the center plate of the truck bolster.

The truck bolster is supported on each end by a series of springs (the spring package), which transfer the weight from the ends of the bolsters to the truck sideframe. The springs cushion the ride and allow the bolster to float up and down depending upon the car's weight.

On early trucks, the springs rested on the ends of the spring plank, a C-shaped channel that ran between the sideframes. Modern trucks eliminated the spring plank (thus the term *plankless* is used to describe many trucks), and instead have the springs sit on a platform cast into each sideframe.

The truck determines the weight capacity of the car, and this is largely a function of the size of the journals and the spring package used. Cars of 40-ton capacity have four or five springs (two visible in front), 50-ton cars use five springs (two visible), and 70-ton cars have seven springs (generally two visible in front, with three springs visible behind).

Some trucks use a *snubber* in place of one of the springs. Snubbers are friction dampers (basically shock absorbers) made in different ways, using flat coiled steel cylinders, rubber blocks, and coil springs, that react in a stiffer manner than a coil spring. Some snubbers replace a coil spring; others are used with a spring located inside the coil. Springs within a package can be of varying stiffness to even out the ride quality.

The full weight of the cars is supported, via the sideframes, on bearings that ride atop the ends of each axle. This area is enclosed by the journal box. Until the 1950s, almost all trucks, such as the one in the drawing, were known as *solid-bearing* (often incorrectly called *friction bearing*).

Because the ends of the axles rotated directly against the journal bearings, the bearings needed constant lubrication. Journal boxes were packed with fibrous cotton material (called *waste*) or pads, and oil was added to the boxes on a regular basis.

In spite of this, bearings often went dry and overheated, causing hotboxes. If not noticed by crew members, a hotbox could result in a fire or even the failure of the bearing, which could cause a wreck.

The solution was the roller-bearing journal, which rolls with much less friction and requires no periodic lubrication. They were significantly more expensive than solid bearings, so railroads were slow to adapt them. They began to appear on some freight equipment in the 1940s and grew in use through the 1950s.

The truck's brake lever is actuated by a rod from the car's brake cylinder. The lever pivots the brake beam, which is held by the brake hanger, to press the brake shoes against the wheel treads.

Early truck types

The most common type of truck into the 1900s was the *archbar*, which had sideframes made of pressed-steel pieces that were bolted together. Although they performed decently, they required constant maintenance to keep bolts tightened. You won't find them on mainline freight cars in the transition era, as they were prohibited from interchange service in 1941.

Trucks having cast sideframes, with the journal boxes cast into the frame, required less maintenance than archbars. The first was developed by the Bettendorf Co., which used a distinctive T-shaped cross section for strength. They were used on new cars into the 1920s.

The T-section truck was superseded by cast sideframes with a U-shaped cross section, which were much stronger. This design was adopted as an American Railway Association (ARA) standard, and later as an Association of

Andrews trucks have a bar below the journal boxes, securing them to the sideframe. This truck has a snubber in place of a coil spring and multi-wear wheels with thick rims.

Vulcan trucks use inverted jaws to secure the separate journal boxes. This truck also has a snubber in place of a coil spring.

Dalman trucks had extra springs outside of the standard spring package. This is a two-level Dalman design. *Trains magazine collection*

American Railroads (AAR) standard, and trucks following this design were built by many manufacturers. They have become known generically—and incorrectly—as Bettendorf trucks.

Each manufacturer's truck designs varied slightly in the shape and angles of the sideframe, the size and shape of the sideframe openings, and the appearance of the end of the bolster. An aid in spotting is the raised lettering on the sideframe, which tells the truck type (ARA or AAR), the design (such as A-3), the manufacturer, and often the railroad and date for which the truck was made.

A variation on early ARA trucks were Andrews and Vulcan trucks, made from around 1910 into the 1930s. Both had cast sideframes— initially with T or L cross sections, eventually setting on the stronger U-shaped cross sections—but they used separate journal boxes that were bolted in place. A selling point at the time was that they saved money by using journal boxes from the archbar trucks they were replacing.

Andrews trucks were more popular (in part, because they were used on all cars ordered by the United States Railroad Administration during World

The National B-1 truck had a distinctive bolster, sideframe, and spring design that were easy to identify. *National Steel Castings*

The most popular truck of the transition era was the ASF A-3 Ride Control, a spring-plankless design. *Lee Langum*

The Barber S-2A was a popular truck from the 1940s into the 1960s. Also a plankless design, it differed from the A-3 in bolster and pedestal design and the shape of the sideframe.

War I). They can be identified by the horizontal steel bar connecting the bottom of each journal box to the sideframe. The top of the journal box is bolted in place.

Vulcan trucks were similar, but used a steel jaw to hold the journal box, creating a distinctive metal fillet between the inside edge of the box and the sideframe.

Andrews and Vulcan trucks could be found on a variety of freight cars through the 1940s, but by the '50s, they had largely been replaced by more modern trucks. Both were banned from interchange service in 1956.

A 1920s attempt to build a truck with improved riding quality was the Dalman truck. Instead of a conventional spring package, the Dalman used six or seven springs on each sideframe, with separate springs just outside the standard spring package. One version of the truck had springs resting on different levels, with the middle springs on the spring plank and the outboard springs on pedestals on the truck sideframe.

Another truck introduced in 1931 was among the first to eliminate the spring plank. The National B-1 had a unique rounded bolster end. The sideframe used an unconventional spring set with long-travel springs tucked inside the sideframe, with two circular openings on the sideframe under the bolster.

Modern truck designs

By the late 1930s, freight cars were getting heavier, trains were growing longer, and train speeds were increasing, so railroads started looking for trucks that provided smoother rides and were more stable, especially at high speeds.

Double-truss trucks were designed to reinforce the area below the spring package on the bottom chord of the sideframe—essentially a second truss to the area where the springs rest. Many makers offered double-truss designs through the 1950s.

Introduced around 1940, the A-3 Ride Control truck from American Steel Foundries (ASF) didn't have a spring plank. The springs instead rested on a pedestal cast integral to the truck sideframe. This truck become the most popular solid-bearing truck into the 1960s.

The Barber S-2, also a new plankless design, was very similar to the ASF truck. It has a slightly different sideframe shape, with a thinner spring pedestal and a different shape at the end of the bolster. The S-2 was also very popular into the 1960s.

It's important to note that from the mid-1930s, manufacturers shared designs and engineering resources through membership in the Four-Wheel Truck Association. Members included American Steel Foundries, Bettendorf, Buckeye, National, Standard Car Truck Co., Symington-Gould, and others. This meant a customer could order an A-3 Ride Control truck from ASF, Buckeye, or Standard.

High-speed trucks were often used on boxcars in express and merchandise service. These were designed with special springs and other devices to control lateral and vertical movement. Among the more common types were the General Steel Castings (GSC) Commonwealth (which looked like a standard passenger-car truck but with a shorter wheelbase), Allied Full Cushion (banned from interchange in 1955 due to operational problems), Symington-Gould double-truss, Symington-Gould Type XL, and the Chrysler. Use of these trucks decreased with the advent of conventional roller-bearing trucks in the 1950s.

Roller bearings

Roller bearings required no lubrication and virtually no maintenance, but their high initial cost kept them from wide use on freight equipment into the transition era.

Roller-bearing trucks can be spotted by rotating end caps on the axle ends. Instead of a journal box, the jaw (an upside-down U shape) holds the roller-bearing adapter, which sits directly atop the axle-end bearing.

Popular early truck sideframes followed the same basic designs as common solid-bearing trucks, including the Barber S-2 and ASF A-3. The truck sideframes generally had a flatter top profile with wider area

The GSC Commonwealth high-speed truck was based on similar passenger-car trucks but with a shorter wheelbase. *Trains magazine collection*

The Allied Full Cushion truck was a unique high-speed truck design with springs surrounding the journal boxes. Derailments led to their being banned from interchange in 1955. *Trains magazine collection*

The Symington-Gould double-truss was a high-speed truck with coil-elliptical springs and a unique sideframe shape, with the top chord dropping down in the middle. *New York Central*

above the axle. End caps varied, with three visible bolt heads surrounded by a raised triangle or hexagon.

Some railroads converted solid-bearing trucks to roller bearings. On these conversions, the adapter was in the journal box. The journal box covers were removed, so the roller-bearing end caps are visible inside the openings.

Although roller-bearing use was increasing by the mid-1950s, especially on high-speed equipment (some reefers and stock cars were early users), they were still not common during the

The journal box holds a pad or cotton waste soaked in oil to lubricate the bearing.

Roller-bearing trucks can be spotted by the end caps, which turn as the car moves. This is a 70-ton ASF Ride Control truck.

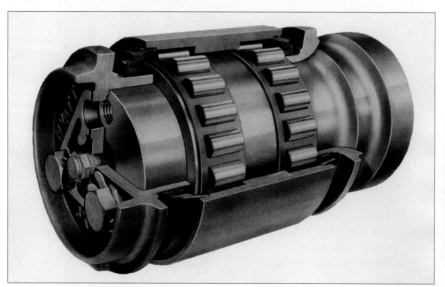

This cutaway view shows how a series of rollers inside the sealed package work to transfer movement from the axle. *Hyatt*

transition era. There were just over 27,000 roller-bearing cars in interchange service in early 1957, barely 1 percent of the total freight car fleet.

Wheels

In the steam era, railroads used two main types of wheels: steel and cast-iron (known as "chilled wheels" for the heat treatment of their treads). Chilled wheels often had ribs cast on the back, to better dissipate the heat generated during braking that could weaken the wheel.

Steel wheels were in common use by the 1920s, and chilled wheels were fading from use by the 1940s. Chilled wheels couldn't be used on new cars after 1957, and they were later banned from interchange service, but that wouldn't happen until 1970.

Wheels were either single-wear (1W) or two-wear (2W). The difference is the rim/tread: 1W rims are 1¼" thick, while 2W wheels are 2", which allows them to be turned (recut) once during their service life.

The most common wheel size is 33" radius, used on almost all cars up

Roller-bearing manufacturers in the 1950s and '60s sold kits to retrofit roller bearings and adapters into the journal boxes on solid-bearing trucks. *Hyatt*

Many chilled wheels had spiral-shaped ribs cast on their backs to better dissipate heat from braking.

Ajax hand brakes were most common and featured distinctive brake wheels having nubs around an inner circle.

Champion wheels were spoked in a spiral pattern with indentations and a solid, concave disk in the center. *Trains magazine collection*

Equipco brake wheels had six spiral spokes coming from the center with an inner ring.

Miner wheels had a center disk and a simple six-spoke pattern with indentations on the outside of the wheel at the spokes.

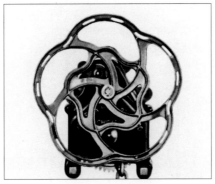

Superior brake wheels had an intricate five-spoke spiral pattern comprising the inner and outer wheels. *Superior*

Universal wheels had a solid disk center with eight spiral spokes going to a smooth outer wheel. *Trains magazine collection*

to 70-ton capacity. Cars of 100-ton capacity have 36"-radius wheels.

Brake equipment

Each freight car has its own set of brake equipment, designed to work with the equipment on all other cars in a train. On some types of cars, such as boxcars, reefers, and flatcars, much of the brake system is hidden underneath the cars. On other car types, such as hoppers, tank cars, and covered hoppers, the brake system is out in the open.

The AB brake system became standard for all new freight cars in 1932 (see drawing on page 92). The train line is the continuous air piping throughout a train formed by connecting air hoses between the cars. A valve at each hose (*angle cock*) can be opened or closed.

Air compressors on a locomotive fill the train line (70 or 90 pounds was common for the transition era). The car's control valve or AB valve

(sometimes incorrectly called a *triple valve*) regulates the air, allowing the reservoir to fill from the train line. The reservoir has separate sections for normal brake applications (service) and emergency applications.

The engineer sets the brakes by releasing air from the train line. The amount of air released triggers the AB valve to transfer a portion of air from the reservoir to the brake cylinder. The piston on the cylinder moves outward and pushes the linkage connected to the trucks, and the linkage then presses the brake shoes against the wheel treads.

In an emergency, the engineer releases all of the air from the train line. This causes all the air, including the emergency portion, to be released from the reservoir to the cylinder. (This is also what happens if the train breaks in two and pulls the air hoses apart.)

On the end of each car is a brake wheel, which is turned to apply and

Handle-style levers were sometimes used, especially where clearance with other car parts was a concern.

release the hand brake. Into the 1930s, brake wheels were generally horizontal atop vertical masts. By the mid-1930s,

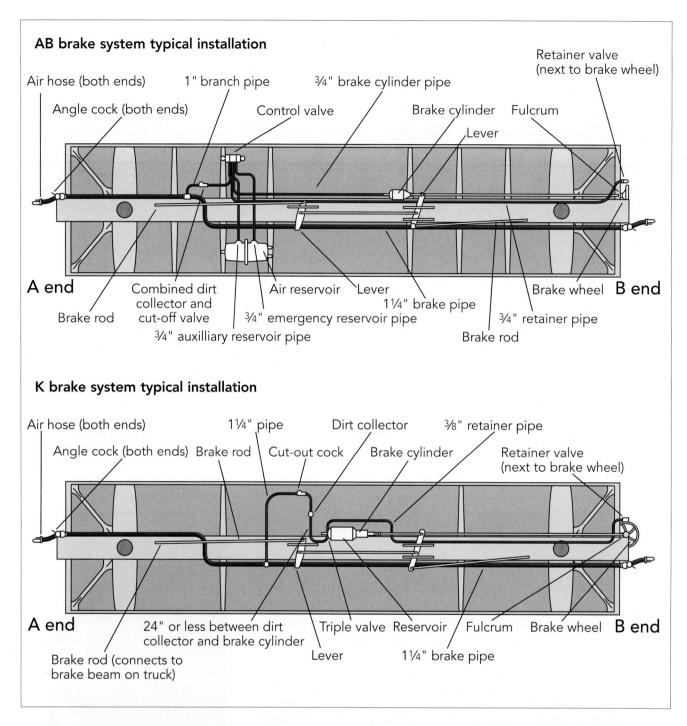

AB brake system typical installation

Retainer valve (next to brake wheel)

Air hose (both ends)   1" branch pipe   ¾" brake cylinder pipe

Angle cock (both ends)   Control valve   Brake cylinder   Fulcrum

Lever

A end

B end

Combined dirt collector and cut-off valve   Air reservoir   Lever

Brake rod   ¾" emergency reservoir pipe   1¼" brake pipe   Brake wheel

¾" auxilliary reservoir pipe   ¾" retainer pipe   Brake rod

K brake system typical installation

Air hose (both ends)   1¼" pipe   Dirt collector   ⅜" retainer pipe

Angle cock (both ends)   Brake rod   Cut-out cock   Brake cylinder   Retainer valve (next to brake wheel)

A end

B end

Brake rod (connects to brake beam on truck)   24" or less between dirt collector and brake cylinder   Triple valve   Reservoir   Fulcrum   Brake wheel

Lever   1¼" brake pipe

geared brake wheels (which provide more control) were common, featuring vertical wheels mounted on a housing.

Brake wheels are a good spotting feature, as manufacturers, including Ajax, Champion, Equipco, Miner, Superior, and Universal, used their own designs, as well as lever-style controls, through the 1950s. An AAR standard design followed.

Also on the end of the car, you'll find the retaining valve next to the brake wheel. This can be set to allow air to

be retained in the brake cylinder even when brakes are released—a common practice when descending steep or long grades. Below the brake wheel and retainer is the brake platform, which provides crewmen a place to stand.

K brakes

Into the 1920s, most cars were equipped with K brakes. The K system worked similarly to the AB system, but it had a slower response time and no separate emergency section in the reservoir. Its

triple valve also had fewer functions than the later AB valve. Components could be coupled together in the K system (called KC for *K combined*), as seen in the drawing above.

K brakes could not be used on new equipment after 1932, and K brakes were banned from interchange traffic in 1953. In the 1940s through 1953, many older cars were converted from K brakes to AB brakes. Check prototype photos of individual cars that you wish to model to make sure.

Bibliography

Boxcars

"AAR 1937 Boxcar Variations," by Martin Lofton, *Mainline Modeler*, October 1991

"ARA 1932 Boxcar," by Martin Lofton, *Mainline Modeler*, Part 1: October 1992, Part 2: November 1992, Part 3: January 1993

"Dominion's Fowler Patent, Single-sheathed Boxcars," by Ted Culotta, *Railroad Model Craftsman*, May 2006

"The Fast Ones: BX Express Boxcars," by Pat Wider, *Railway Prototype Cyclopedia*, Vol. 6

"The 50-foot Boxcar, Part 4: AAR-style Single Door Cars Circa 1941-1959," by Jim Eager, *RailModel Journal*, June 1990

Focus on Freight Cars, Vol. 1: Single-sheathed Box and Automobile Cars, by Richard Hendrickson. Speedwitch Media, 2006

"40-foot Cryogenic Gas Box/Tank Cars," by Pat Wider, *Railway Prototype Cyclopedia*, Vol. 14

"40-foot Double-door Boxcars," by Ed Hawkins, *RailModel Journal*, June 1992

"40-foot Single-door Boxcars, 1955-1961," by Ed Hawkins, *RailModel Journal*, August 1992

"40-foot Single-sheathed Z-Braced Boxcars," by Richard Hendrickson, *RailModel Journal*, February 1993

"Fowler Boxcar," by Jeffrey M. Koeller, *Mainline Modeler*, August 1992

"The Mather Boxcar," Martin Lofton, *Railroad Model Craftsman*, February 1991

"Milwaukee Ribbed-side Boxcar," by Kirk Reddie, *Mainline Modeler*, Part 1: June 1988, Part 2: September 1988

"Milwaukee Road Ribbed-Side Box and Automobile Cars," by Pat Wider, *Railway Prototype Cyclopedia*, Vol. 13

"Modeler's Guide to Steel Boxcars," by Tony Koester, *Model Railroader*, May 2006

"Modeling Riveted 40-foot PS-1 Boxcars with Six-foot Doors," by Pat Wider and Ed Hawkins, *Railway Prototype Cyclopedia*, Vol. 1

"Modified 1937 AAR 40-foot Cars," by Ed Hawkins, *RailModel Journal*, August 1996

"Murphy Ends," by John Nehrich, *Mainline Modeler*, December 1986

"1932 ARA Standard Steel Boxcar," by John Nehrich, *Mainline Modeler*, February 1986

"Pennsy X32: Their First 50-foot Boxcar," *Mainline Modeler*, October 1990

"Pennsylvania RR X29 and ARA 40-foot Steel-sheathed Boxcars," by Richard Hendrickson, *RailModel Journal*, December 2001

"Pennsylvania X29B," by Martin Lofton, *Mainline Modeler*, December 1992

"Pullman's 50-foot PS-1," by Jeffrey M. Koeller, *Mainline Modeler*, July 1993

"Shippers' Delight Boxcar" (GAEX 50-foot cars), *Railway Age*, April 22, 1950

"Standard Boxcars, 1920s to PS-1," by Martin Lofton, *Mainline Modeler*, April 1993

"Standard Boxcars, 1930s to PS-1," by Martin Lofton, *Mainline Modeler*, May 1993

"Steel-side USRA Rebuilds, Part 1," by Martin Lofton, *Railroad Model Craftsman*, September 1989

"10'-0" Inside Height Postwar 40'-6" AAR Boxcars," by Ed Hawkins, *Railway Prototype Cyclopedia*, Vol. 8

"USRA Double-sheathed Rebuilds," by John Nehrich, *Mainline Modeler*, June 1988

"USRA 40-foot Single-sheathed Boxcars," by Stephen Priest, *Scale Rails*, December 2006

"War Emergency Boxcars," by Richard Hendrickson, *Mainline Modeler*, Part 1: August 1994, Part 2: September 1994

"X29 Boxcar," by Ben Hom, *Mainline Modeler*, Part 1: August 2004, Part 2: September 2004

Refrigerator cars

"American Car & Foundry's 1920s Wood Refrigerator Cars," by Ted Culotta, *Railroad Model Craftsman*, April 2006

"American Refrigerator Transit Early Steel Refrigerator Cars," by Richard Hendrickson, *RailModel Journal*, June 2007

"American Refrigerator Transit 40- and 42-foot Wooden Reefers," by Al Westerfield, *RailModel Journal*, March 1992

"Canadian Railways' Refrigerator Cars," by A. N. Campbell, *Railway Age*, June 17, 1950

The Great Yellow Fleet, by John H. White. Golden West Books, 1986

"History of ART Refrigerator Cars," by Gene Semon, *Model Railroading*, March 1989

"Meat Reefers," by Martin Lofton, *Mainline Modeler*. Part 1: February 1992, Part 2: March 1992, Part 3: April 1992

"Mechanical Cooling Pays Its Way," by C. B. Peck, *Railway Age*, April 18, 1955

Pacific Fruit Express, Second Edition, by Anthony W. Thompson et. al., Signature Press, 2000

"Reefers of the Union Refrigerator Transit Co.," by Al Westerfield, *RailModel Journal*, July 1992

"Reefers, Stock Cars, and Tank Cars of the Swift Fleet," by Martin Lofton, *RailModel Journal*, February 1993

Refrigerator Cars, Ice Bunker Cars 1884-1979 (Santa Fe), by Richard H. Hendrickson et. al., Santa Fe Modelers Organization Inc., 1994

"Santa Fe's Rebuilt USRA Reefers," by Ted Culotta, *Railroad Model Craftsman*, August 2006

"They're Built to Maintain Zero" (Northern Pacific mechanical cars), *Railway Age*, April 25, 1955

Hoppers and gondolas

"ACF 70-ton Hart Selective Service Ballast Cars," by Pat Wider, *Railway Prototype Cyclopedia*, Vol. 3

"The AAR 70-ton Hopper," by Robert L. Hundman, *Mainline Modeler*, December 1990

"The Anthracite Roads' Fishbelly Hoppers," by John Nehrich, *RailModel Journal*, February 1992

"ARA Standard 70-ton Quadruple Hopper Cars," by Ed Hawkins, *Railway Prototype Cyclopedia*, Vol. 5

"52'-6" Drop-end De Facto Standard 70-ton Mill Gondola, by Ed Hawkins and John Spencer, *Railway Prototype Cyclopedia*, Vol. 3

"The Minnesota Ore Car," by Pat Dorin and Jeff Koeller, *Mainline Modeler*, December 2003

"1935 50/60-ton AAR Two-bay Offset Hopper, 1934-1960," by Ed Hawkins, *Railway Prototype Cyclopedia*, Vol. 1

"Offset-side Hopper: The ARA/AAR Standards," by Robert L. Hundman, *Mainline Modeler*, September 1987

"Ore Cars," by Patrick Dorin, *Mainline Modeler*, September 1994

"Panel-Side Hopper Cars," by John Nehrich, *Mainline Modeler*, January 1990

"PS-3 Hopper," by Robert L. Hundman," *Mainline Modeler*, November 1998

"Santa Fe Caswell Drop-bottom Gondolas," by Richard Hendrickson, *RailModel Journal*, December 2006

"Stewart Hobbies HO 40-foot, 3-bay Hoppers, by Jim Eager, *RailModel Journal*, January 1991

"USRA Composite Gondola," by R. H. Hendrickson, *Prototype Modeler*, August 1979

"USRA 70-ton Hopper Car," by Keith Thompson, *Model Railroader*, October 1992

"USRA Twin Hoppers," by Richard Hendrickson, *RailModel Journal*, May 1995

"War Emergency Hopper," by Robert L. Hundman, *Mainline Modeler*, January 1997

Tank cars

"ACF Tank Cars," by Cyril Durrenberger, *Mainline Modeler*, December 1993

"ACF 3-dome Tank Cars," by John Riddell, *Mainline Modeler*, September 1995

"ACF Type 21 Tank Cars," by Richard Hendrickson, *RailModel Journal*, February 1998

"ACF Type 21 Tank Cars, Part 2," by Richard Hendrickson, *RailModel Journal*, January 2000

"ACF Type 27 ICC-103 10,000-gallon Tank Cars," by Richard Hendrickson, *RailModel Journal*, July 1997

"ACF Type 27, 10,500-gallon, ICC-105A Propane Tank Cars," by Ed Hawkins, *Railway Prototype Cyclopedia*, Vol. 7

"ACF 8,000-gallon Riveted Tank Cars," by Richard Hendrickson, *RailModel Journal*, October 1997

"Fifities-era Welded Tank Cars," by Richard Hendrickson, *RailModel Journal*, April 1996

"ICC-105, 11,000-gallon High-pressure Tank Cars," by Richard Hendrickson, *RailModel Journal*, July 2003

"Modeler's Guide to Transition-era Tank Cars," by Tony Koester, *Model Railroader*, December 2008

"6,000-gallon Insulated High-pressure Tank Cars from Trix Models" (ACF), by Richard M. Hendrickson, *RailModel Journal*, September 2004

Steam Era Freight Cars Reference Manual, Vol. 2: Tank Cars, Speedwitch Media, 2008

"Union Tank Car Co. 10,000-gallon Class X-3 Tank Car" (drawing), *Mainline Modeler*, March 1985

Covered hoppers

"ACF 70-ton Covered Hoppers," *RailModel Journal*, April 1991

"ACF Two-bay LOs and Clones," *RailModel Journal*, May 1994

"Airslide Covered Hoppers," by Bill McKean, *Mainline Modeler*, December 1986

"Carbon Black," by Martin Lofton, *Mainline Modeler*, May 1993

"Covered Hoppers Class LO," *Railway Age*, June 30, 1934

"Greenville GV-2 Covered Hopper Car," by Ed Hawkins, *Railway Prototype Cyclopedia*, Vol. 3

"PS-2 Covered Hopper," *Mainline Modeler*, September 1998

"PS-2 Covered Hoppers," by James Eager, *RailModel Journal*, June 1992

"PS-2 Covered Hoppers," by Martin Lofton, *Mainline Modeler*. Part 1: July 1991, Part 2: August 1991, Part 3: November 1991

"70-ton Phosphate Quadruple Covered Hopper Cars," by Pat Wider, *Railway Prototype Journal*, Vol. 4

"2,600-cubic-foot Airslide Covered Hopper Cars (1953-1959)," by Ed Hawkins, *Railway Prototype Cyclopedia*, Part 1: Vol. 17, Part 2: Vol. 20, Part 3: Vol. 22

"Pennsylvania H30A Covered Hoppers," by C. R. Yungkurth, *Model Railroader*, October 1981

Flatcars

"Commonwealth Cast Steel Flatcars," by James Eager, *RailModel Journal*, December 1992

"53'-6" 50-ton AAR Flatcars," by Richard Hendrickson, *Model Railroading*, December 1988

Intermodal Railroading, by Brian Solomon. Voyageur Press/MBI, 2007

"Pennsylvania F30 Flatcar with Fabricated Frame," by Martin Lofton, *Mainline Modeler*, December 1991

"Pennsy's Truc-Train F39A Flatcar," *Railroad Model Craftsman*, July 1990

"USRA-design 42-foot Flatcars," by Richard Hendrickson, *RailModel Journal*, January 1997

Stock cars

"B&O's Mather Stock Car," *Mainline Modeler*, September 1987

"C&NW Stock Car: 1950s Rebuilds," by Jeffrey M. Koeller, *Mainline Modeler*, November 2003

"Harriman Standard (UP/SP/WP) 36-foot Stock Cars," by Richard Hendrickson, *RailModel Journal*, October 2006

Stock Car Cyclopedia, Vol. 1, by Robert L. Hundman. Hundman Publishing, 2007

"Stock Cars," by John Nehrich, *Mainline Modeler*, Part 1: June 1990, Part 2: July 1990, Part 3: August 1990

General information

"Arch Bars to Roller Bearings: Freight Car Trucks 1900-1960," by Richard Hendrickson, *Railway Prototype Cyclopedia*, Vol. 4

"Freight Car Running Boards and Brake Steps," by Ed Hawkins, *Railway Prototype Cyclopedia*, Vol. 16

"Making the Connection" (Couplers), by Richard Dawson, *Trains*, August 2000

Car Builders' Cyclopedia, various editions

Official Railway Equipment Register, various editions

About the author

Jeff Wilson has written more than 30 books on railroads and model railroading. He spent 10 years as an associate editor at *Model Railroader* magazine, and he currently works as a freelance writer, editor, and photographer, contributing articles to MR and other magazines.

He enjoys many facets of the hobby, especially building structures and detailing locomotives, as well as photographing both real and model railroads.

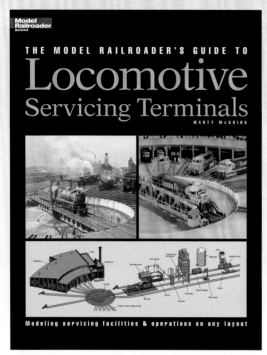
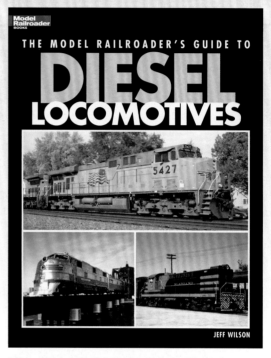